I0149493

ABOUT THE AUTHOR

Following graduation from USAF Bombardier School, David Irvin was assigned to the 447th Bomb Group of the 8th Air Force. In November of 1943, his B-17 was shot down and he was captured by the Germans. Undaunted, Irvin escaped and traveled through Belgium and Denmark and was returned to his unit courtesy of a State Department aircraft flying out of Sweden. He completed 30 combat missions and then returned to the US to complete his pilot training.

In 1948, Irvin volunteered for the Berlin Airlift and flew 185 missions from Rhein-Main AB at Frankfurt, Germany. He later volunteered in the B-47 program and completed training in navigation, radar, and bombardier school (again) to become what is respectively known as a "4-headed monster" in the Air Force. Assigned to the 9th Bomb Wing, he pulled temporary duty in Guam and flew missions over North Korea.

Other assignments include duty with 44th Bomb wing and 2nd AF HQ in Louisiana. In 1964, Irvin was transferred to Strategic Air Command HQ where he served for four years on detached service, and he flight tested the Lockheed U-2R in Vietnam. He was then transferred to the 14th Strategic Aerospace Division at Beale AFB in California where he was the SR71 project officer and division special project officer.

Special Operations is a true story documenting the short range history of the bomber force. Told in three parts, it demonstrates the versatility of the military pilot and observer and is a credit to the training they received, coupled with the experience each one of them acquired.

OTHER BOOKS BY COLONEL IRVIN:

Reconnaissance Is Black

Escape or Evade

Highway to Freedom

SPECIAL
OPERATIONS

Colonel David W. Irvin, Jr.

TURNER PUBLISHING COMPANY

TURNER PUBLISHING COMPANY

Copyright © 2002 Colonel David W. Irwin, Jr.
Publishing Rights: Turner Publishing Company

Turner Publishing Company Staff:
Publishing Consultant: Virginia-Sue Forstot
Designer: Susan L. Harwood

Library of Congress Control No: 2002104681

ISBN: 978-1-68162-397-9

Additional copies may be purchased
directly from the publisher.
Limited Edition

TABLE OF CONTENTS

PROLOGUE

This story is in three parts and demonstrates the versatility of the military pilot and observer and is a credit to the training they received, coupled with the experience each one of them acquired. First, the reader will learn how the novice military pilot was prepared for his introduction to the jet bomber. It is necessarily direct and still leads the reader along the route of what goes into the preparation each crew member goes through and ultimately becomes a professional. Part two is the explicit training the crew members go through to become a neophyte in the strategic bomber force that can and will, defend our nation, if the need arises. Each aircraft, in this advanced technological age of flight, has a specific purpose and to use it in other than its designed role and the trained crew is a travesty, a waste of money and individual expertise.

The concept of high level flight technique for penetrating enemy defenses originated in WWII, initially and then progressed into higher altitude bombing and like any other advances, brought us into the jet age. The manufacture of the jet bomber, powered by jet engines, was a change of philosophy that rivaled the nuclear bomb, and we all should know how that changed the complexities of warfare. Thus was borne the global and limited war concept. Under each condition, the concept of high altitude technique was the approved philosophy that was perpetuated, until the introduction of the Surface-to-Air (SAM) missile. Because of the initial inherent inaccuracy of the SAM, the high altitude penetration bomber approach still remained in effect. Within the space of five years, approximately, the accuracy of the foreign missiles dramatically changed the strategic bombing concept. We were literally forced to go into a low level high speed mode. The Boeing Stratojet (B-47) was conceived and manufactured with the continued idea of high altitude bombing. We were all trained in the high altitude approach, but SAC had a problem and they did the best they could to change from high to low altitude. Unfortunately, none of the pilots, observers or planners were trained to fly the bomber at speeds and altitudes never considered in all of their previous training.

Part three demonstrates the abrupt change to low altitude and high speed penetrations of enemy territory. The National Authority still considered high altitude as the initial phase, followed by aerial refueling and making the bomb run at unfamiliar attitudes and speeds was to be overcome by practice, practice and refinement.

One huge problem remained and it was not to be taken without exposing the flight crew and airplane to a nuclear blast. The problem was one of releasing the nuclear weapon and being able to escape the explosion. The nuclear experts, primarily at Sandia Base, near Albuquerque, New Mexico finally solved the problem, they thought, of the only escape route that could provide somewhat of a safety factor for the people who released the weapon. It must be remembered this was the real reason for all of the preparation. The crews knew it and were prepared to do what needed to be done if a nuclear conflict was a reality. Thus was borne the "Pop-Up" maneuver, as it was called. A detailed explanation will be covered in the late chapters of this book. Suffice it to say, this was the ultimate hazard the flight crews would be expected to do. In the 1950-1960s there were no technological wonders that allowed a small nuclear weapon to be launched from enough distance to allow the crew to escape to safety.

The method of training the bomber crews for a low level high speed approach was hastily conceived and became an immediate operational/training problem for the testing of the new idea. How this evolved will be explained and should surprise the reader. The idea was not novel, but expedient. Fortunately, we did not lose any B-47s, but when introduced to the B-52 fleet (the successor to the B-47 and also built by Boeing) the low level techniques caused the loss of several of the eight-engine behemoths.

In retrospect, the strategic planners really had a difficult decision as to how to get the crews into the mode of the concept of flying a big bomber at extremely low altitudes and high speeds.

This story is without an ending, happily or not. The Strategic Air Command (SAC) and the Tactical Air Command (TAC) were integrated into the Strike Command. On the strategic side of the ledger, the late model B-52s (G and H model), the B-1 and B-2 are the backbone of the long range force. Fortunately, they don't have a mission and hopefully, will not be needed. With that in mind the short range history of the bomber force will be historically documented source for our children to learn and understand.

Fortunately, Operation Texas League was without any fatalities, due exclusively to the expertise, knowledge and aggression of the flight crews, both tanker and bomber. Although the exercise was accomplished when the Cold War was in full operation, the dedication of the young men of the Air Force demonstrated their support of following the dictums of higher authority.

On the other hand, Operation Whiskey Orange sustained losses, but proved the flexibility of aircraft and crews that continued to support the National Objectives.

In the annals of aviation the exploits of legendary pioneers are called to mind, Orville and Wilbur Wright, Charles Lindbergh, Amelia Earhart, Hap Arnold, Curtis LeMay and others bring memories of the dynamic people who furthered the cause of manned flight. There are others, who made singular contributions but are unheralded because of circumstances, nevertheless deserve to be remembered because, without them, the expansion of the airplane would never had been perpetuated.

This story is true in every respect. The dates, places, circumstances and events actually happened. The names, their deeds and misdeeds should not be acknowledged except for what they did and not who did them. The embarrassment caused by the results of poor planning, faulty execution and lack of leadership points out how individual effort can overcome insurmountable odds.

Special Operations is dedicated to the professional military aviators, who are too often maligned during peacetime, but taken for granted in times of conflict.

A B-47E without wing tanks. The white paint was not standard and was not on SAC B-47s.

Chapter 1

THE OPERATIONAL CONCEPT

From the late 1940s, the Strategic Air Command (SAC) used the B-29 (from WWII use), the B-50 and B-36 as its front-line bomber force. The Cold War was beginning to pressure both the United States and Russia to "compete" for domination for the strategic aircraft forces. The missiles had not made their appearance, but the Russians were forced into a defensive position and started producing the best front-line tactical jets aircraft.

The United States was still using the North American P-51 (the best fighter in WWII) and pressure on the aircraft industry to expand the F-86 and retool for advanced tactical aircraft. The British were using the Meteor jet, but the French and Canadians were still far behind.

For some inexplicable reason the Russians never had a front-line bomber force. Instead, they were to advance their position by manufacturing the Surface-to-Air (SAM) missile. Their concept forced the Allies to change their strategic thinking. The tactical aircraft were not in jeopardy in the 1950s. What the United States needed was a strategic jet bomber, capable of carrying a 20,000 pound nuclear bomb. Our prop-driven bombers could and the B-36 (with eight propeller pusher engines and four jet engines for use on takeoff and climb) could be very slow bombers, too slow to outrun or battle the Russian fighters (MiG-15 and successors).

Airborne radar was out of its infancy. We had invented advanced radar, learned from the British in 1944-45, as used in their Pathfinder Force (PFF). It was crude and its accuracy was circumspect, but much better than night visual bombing strikes on German targets. Our piston bombers were using radar bombing techniques, but it was not accurate enough for the present-day strategic forces.

Although still needing refinement, our airborne radar was becoming more and more sophisticated and was ready for the newest bomber in the Air Force inventory, the Boeing B-47 jet aircraft, particularly, but they had one strategic disadvantage. They burned fuel at an alarming rate at low altitudes. As a comparison, the twin engine B-25 burned 100 gallons per hour, or 640 pounds. The B-47 burned 1,565 gallons (10,000 pounds) per hour at low altitudes. The jets burned JP4 fuel. That means a refinement of piston-driven engines aviation gas (115 octane) was refined four times further for the jet to operate at peak efficiency. The jet engine would be able to burn AVGAS but was not efficient. This consumption was reduced above 30,000 feet to 6,000 pounds (640 gallons per hour), a significant reduction considering the B-47 could take-off with a maximum of 80,000 pounds without wing tanks.

In case the reader is wondering why the weight of the fuel is critical when flying jets, the jet engine is very inefficient while on the ground and at low level. Therefore, weight is critical and take-off and landing speeds must be exceptionally precise. The pilot under optimum conditions, flies the approach (to landing) at five knots (six mph) above stall, for one reason: the jets land faster than prop-driven planes because of the required air flow, thus the landing distance can be a big problem.

The reason for such a detailed explanation of jet operation is to acquaint and indoctrinate the reader to the inherent exposure the pilot has in flying a large multi-engine jet bomber. It may surprise the reader to understand that landing a multi-engine jet at heavy weights is much easier than landing at light weights. The reason is simple. At heavy weights, big jets approach the runway at faster speeds. At flareout, once the aircraft in landing altitude and the engines are retarded to idle, the aircraft immediately loses lift and will land and not "float," as it does at light weights.

Recognize that since SAC became a strategic retaliatory force, the sole emphasis has been high altitude response as it was during WWII. This was predicated on the hard fact that our new jet bomber force (B-47) could fly above the anti-aircraft guns and could extend their range at high altitude. To augment this strike force, Boeing was manufacturing the C-97, four propeller transport that would be modified to carry fuel for the bombers. This was done by way of a telescoping boom fitted beneath the tail. A refueling operator controlling the boom, was redesignated a KC-97 and training was accomplished at Randolph AFB, San Antonio, Texas. The crew had a pilot, copilot, navigator and boom operator. The pilots initially come from the B-29 force.

The first B-47s were sent to the 305th and 306th Bomb Wings located at MacDill AFB, Tampa, Florida. The training was intense and crews primarily learned as they flew. I distinctly remember sitting in a B-25 twin engine light bomber, turned into a transport after WWII, and was told to hold my engine start by the tower at Kirtland AFB, Albuquerque, New Mexico. The tower then announced there would be no take-offs or landings, that an experimental plane was on final approach. I looked out and saw a strange looking aircraft, drooping wings, multi-engines and coming fast. As the plane crossed the end of the runway, I could see a plastic canopy, outriggers below the inboard engines and what seemed like it was in landing position before it flared before touchdown. When it landed, a large parachute blossomed from the tail noticeably slowing the aircraft. The date was January 9, 1949 and I was looking at the XB-47B on a test flight from Edwards AFB in the desert of southern California. Little did I know I was going to fly the bird three years later. I was fortunate to take a picture of the "monster." Still have it, a treasured memento.

Chapter 2

Concentrated Training

When I returned from flying the Berlin Airlift in 1949, I was assigned to Sheppard AFB, Wichita Falls, Texas. Not exciting.

At first I was content flying B-25s, AT-6s and C-45s but then I saw a training command call for pilots who wanted to fly the new B-47 for SAC. There would be a nine-month training program before being able to fly America's first multi-jet strategic bomber.

The B-47 had a three-man crew (aircraft commander, pilot and radar/navigator), a radical departure from the WWII B-17 (nine men), to the B-29 (9-10 men). This change required each crew member to do the work of three. By far, the radar/navigator/bombardier had the heaviest load, but they were compensated for by the copilot, who as a trained navigator, would operate the sextant as coordinated by the navigator. Quite often the copilot and navigator would pre-compute (on the ground) the stars to be used on the celestial leg of the forthcoming flight. The pilot (called aircraft commander in SAC) would plot the route to be flown on aeronautical charts and included emergency runways of 8,000 feet in length along the route, SAC Command Post call signs, turning points and other things he wanted to be annotated.

The pilot would normally make the radio calls, freeing the copilot and navigator to coordinate without interruption. By far the most critical coordination between the crew members was during aerial refueling. More about that later.

During the celestial navigation by the navigator and the copilot closely coordinated between stars to be "shot," timing and "shot" results. There were three separate shots and the navigator plotted each of them and used them to determine the aircraft's location. The last "fix" was used to determine the heading to be flown to reach the predetermined destination.

All of this was done without use of radar, in case it would be exposed to failure, or if the flight was over water. While conducting a celestial navigation leg, the copilot had to get out of his ejection seat for at least nine minutes and this was not one to be contemplated. On top of the celestial activity he had to check the fuel consumption by coordinating with the pilot, but not during the time of "shooting" the stars. He also had to check hydraulic pressures and electrical readings. He was busy to say the least.

While preparing for a simulated bomb run, the pilot made the radio calls, the copilot read the bombing checklist (four pages), while the radar/navigator checked and tuned the radar system, fine-tuning as he approached the target (to give him maximum clarity) and searched for the target area. Once he identifies the specific target, he asks for control of the aircraft, the aircraft being under control of the auto-pilot and monitored by the pilot.

Before operationally going from 40,000 feet to 500 feet, perhaps the most exhilarating part of the mission profile was aerial refueling. The proximity of another aircraft, the precise maneuvering, the flow of fuel, the time-consuming onload of fuel, all of these were exhausting, but the feeling of accomplishment overshadows everything else.

Aerial refueling, the early days (1950) was between the B-47 and the KC-97 at 15-17,000 feet at 170 knots. When the KC-135 (with four jet engines) became operational and was added to the strategic force, refueling was at 20-25,000 feet at 250 knots. Fuel flow using the KC-135 was about twice that of the prop-driven tanker. As the "receiver" (as the bomber was called) electronically came within range (about 90 miles), the B-47 started to descend at 280 knots. As the B-47 passes through the KC-97s altitude, a turbulent feeling from the prop of the tanker is felt. Pre-determined tanker altitude was briefed on the ground, so the receiver leveled off 500 feet below the tanker altitude.

All the time the B-47 radar operator calls off distances (as reflected on his radar). The level-off normally puts the receiver five miles behind the tanker. The B-47s throttles have been in idle (40 percent thrust) and the airspeed is reducing. As an example, I looked up and there it was. The navigator said "four miles" and the copilot said "180." I advanced all six throttles to about 65 percent and the rate of closure was good, the boom was in the trail position, extended. "Two miles," "185" and I could see the boomer in his position. "Open refueling door," I said and the copilot, who by this time had control of the fuel panel, opened the door, slowing the speed by five knots. There was the sound of rushing air and I could see the door was open. "Ready for contact," said the copilot as the boom operator moved the boom up and down, signifying he was ready for contact. I moved into the observation position then advanced the throttles slightly. The aircraft slid into refueling position. I glanced at the boom director lights (on the underside of the belly of the tanker) that said "up," "down," "in," "out" and the color "green," that indicated being in the proper position.

The envelope was four feet left or right, four feet up and six feet down. Imagine the hood of your car and that is about the space you can move 170,000 pounds and not get an automatic disconnect. Remember, a disconnect causes overuse of fuel. It can get real critical when trying to extend your flight.

Once the off-load has been received (or time has expired, or distance has run out), the boom operator rattles the boom and the receiver pilot pushes the disconnect button and retards the throttles, letting the aircraft move back and dropping the nose. When there is enough space between the two aircraft, the bomber pilot advances all six engines and lets the aircraft accelerate and starts to climb (to the left or right), while the copilot closes the refueling door and makes note of the fuel indicators. The navigator announces the heading to fly and the copilot advises of the onload and total fuel aboard, then returns control of the fuel panel to the pilot.

Chapter 3

THE ROAD TO THE B-47

I applied for the B-47 training during Christmas 1950. I got my orders to report to Ellington AFB outside of Houston, Texas in February 1951.

The intense navigator training was interesting. It was exactly the same training the young aviation cadets underwent to get their second lieutenant bars. There was a humorous side before we "graduated" in September 1951. There were 30 officers in our class, almost all of us combat veterans of WWII, some lieutenants and some captains. All of us were pilots, most with a minimum of 2,000 pilot flying hours (the requirement to apply for the training). The instructors were mostly young lieutenants with no previous training or experience and most of them didn't know how to handle us. We made it easy for them. We behaved ourselves and worked hard to assimilate the ground and air training.

All of us graduated and received our orders to report to Mather AFB, Sacramento, California. We started bombardier training "learning" about the Norden bombsight. I never understood why we went through this phase of training for we never were to use the Norden sight, the B-47 optical and radar bombing did not use the WWII instrument. Theory, I suppose was the idea, to acquaint the pilots with bombing.

Our graduation was not full of pomp and ceremony, but we got our orders to stay at Mather and receive our radar training. The bombing phase of training was humorous, because I graduated from Bombardier School at Deming Army Air Base in New Mexico in January 1943 and flew 30 missions for the 8th Air Force in England, was a Prisoner of War, escaped and returning to my unit to complete my tour of combat duty. When I came back I underwent pilot training. Now I was going back to how I started. It was a job dropping the same practice bombs I did in training in 1943; this time from a B-25 on the bombing range at Beale AFB, northeast of Sacramento.

When we weren't bombing, we were piloting the B-25 and immediately started in Radar School. No transfer this time. The last phase of our training was in airborne radar, flying the Lockheed T-29 twin-engine transport. Again, this was a very concentrated course. I found operating the radar a fascinating subject. The ground returns, as portrayed by the electronic system, required a certain amount of thought in determining what cities will look like on the radar scope. The definition (like focusing your television set), it needs tuning to obtain maximum clarity.

Our class graduated June 26, 1952 and we each received certificates announcing we were now Aircraft Observers, Bombardment (AOB). We also received our assignments. As somewhat of a surprise, we "new" AOBs were scattered all over the United States, but only to SAC bases. None of the bases had, or would receive the B-47 in the near future. My assignment was at nearby Travis AFB to the 9th Bombardment Wing. Their unit flew B-29s and consisted of the 1st, 5th and 99th Bomb Squadrons.

Upon arrival at Travis, I was assigned to the 5th Squadron that happened to be on SAC overseas rotation to Anderson AFB, Guam in the Mariana Island chain for a 90-day period. There being nothing to do, I talked to the base operations officer and he agreed to let me fly the T-11, T-7, C-47 and B-25. The squadron was glad to get rid of its "orphan" until the squadron returned. Flying three to four times per week was invigorating and I was very happy to be back in the air again.

It was at this time, having little to do, I nosed around Wing Operations and learned that the reason for us not going directly into the B-47 units was because at Boeing and MacDill AFB, the B-47B was experiencing fuel and electrical problems. Boeing was running four months behind on delivery dates (60 aircraft) and MacDill had grounded 40 percent of the B-47Bs. To say the least, Air Force, SAC and Boeing were going crazy trying to find the causes. The production line had stopped, but the Training Command kept cranking out AOBs, all of which was getting more and more backed up.

Boeing engineers finally traced the fuel leak problems. It was a subcontractor making faulty brass fittings. They were replaced, thus ending the leaking fuel. The electrical problem was traced to a weak circuit breaker. Fixed by replacement and by January 1953, the production line started up again and thus the B-47Es were received by the next units to convert from B-29s to B-47s. The backlog of AOBs had not decreased and the Pinecastle training unit was full so there was a natural disparity in aircraft and crews. All of this kept the B-29/B-50 in the active force inventory. While the B-29 units scheduled to convert to the B-47 gave the new AOBs experience in SAC operations, the problem of filling crew slots was aggravated by the loss of AOBs to the converting units. This went on from January to April 1952 when the squadron returned from overseas. The crews were allowed two weeks to "recover." The planes needed a lot of work and the Wing Maintenance had their hands full. The engines had been overworked, due to the high humidity and temperatures while on Guam.

During the mid-April time period I flew 22 times and got the pilot skills back when the squadron off-duty time was canceled. There was a daily meeting in the squadron briefing room. I initially was assigned to a Combat Ready crew as bombardier. It was during this time period two things happened: the new AOBs were assigned to fill the empty crew spaces and we were told to expect to be at Travis for about a year. This was particularly frustrating because we would not be able to keep our specialties current.

To digress, SAC had a special promotion system separate from the rest of the Air Force. Specifically, its bomber flight crews started as non-ready (NC), nine specialists together needing to mold themselves into a cohesive and coordinated crew. When they had been together for a specified time and completed successfully day and night navigation, radar and optical simulated bombing, gunnery, live bomb drops and many day and night take-offs and landings. When all this was completed, a standardization crew would test each crew member and then declare the crew as combat ready, contingent upon the squadron and wing commander's approval.

Besides having no longer to fly with instructors, the new crew was assigned a foreign target (selected by the Pentagon), in most cases a target within the periphery of the enemy country, such places as airfields, ships/docks and secondary-type targets.

Once the combat ready crew had been flying together and demonstrated a successful series of bombing techniques, day/night celestial navigation, including special emphasis on polar navigation, and the crew has performed a SAC rotation (in case of the 9th Bomb Wing that was Guam and Tokyo) and has completed various ground and air tasks, only then can the squadron commander recommend the crew be selected to the status of lead crew. The wing operations officer and wing commander, if they all agree, the crew must be flight and ground tested (including nuclear weapon loading) by the SES (Strategic Evaluation Squadron), located at MacDill AFB. Their evaluation is the most thorough, vigorous and intensive that can be done in three flights from MacDill. If, at the end of these flights and ground testing, the crew has successfully passed, they are declared as a lead crew.

After the new lead crew returns to Travis, they were assigned a priority foreign target. They are required to review, every 90 days, the route, the target and the withdrawal, including application the every-changing seasonal wind structure.

The bombardier and radar operator are the main players in this profile with the navigator being a close second in priority. Upon their return, the squadron commander organizes a party at the Officers Club and the Airmen's Mess. It is a custom that has lost its touch over the years.

The last rung on the crew ladder was select crew status. This was more of a political, as well as financial status not achieved by more than 10 percent of the B-29, B-50 and B-36 crew force. By my being assigned to a combat ready crew, kept its integrity and status, I did my part by getting good scores on simulated targets in San Francisco, Los Angeles and Phoenix. The B-29 was stable if controlled and trimmed properly. Unfortunately, we were using the Mark 7 Norden bombsight and that reduced its accuracy because its stability was not the greatest, but it was better than, by score comparison, most of the squadron bombardiers.

Since April 1952, I had flown with the combat ready crew. Lt. Kiminau was the aircraft commander. In June I was transferred to a select crew commanded by Lt. Col. Bill Greenwald, a long-time B-29 pilot, but not in WWII. I had a long talk with the squadron commander, Maj. Holsey and he advised me Greenwald needed a highly qualified bombardier to "protect" his crew "spot" promotions. Their bombardier had left the Air Force. This left the crew spot promotions in jeopardy and he told me he knew I was "under the gun," but felt my background was solid and that I could do the job. Good pressure speech. Greenwald had been promoted from major, his navigator was promoted to major, his flight engineer was promoted to master sergeant, his radar operator was elevated to lieutenant colonel and his tail gunner/boom operator was now a technical sergeant. The crew had been together for three years and held the top spot in the squadron. Holsey reiterated he was taking a chance by putting me on an experienced select crew, but the aircraft commander said he believed I could do the job and asked for my comments.

Before I could say anything, he added the crew was scheduled to go through their annual SES profile. That really put the pressure on me. For all intents and purposes, I held the crew spot promotions in the balance. I told the CO I would take the transfer for I had a lot of confidence in my abilities and felt I could hold my own with any bombardier they could throw at me. It was not ego, for I knew what to expect and felt they put their pants on one leg at a time and so could I.

One consideration I had to have assurances I would get maximum pilot time, the AC was an instructor pilot that allowed him to spread the pilot/copilot time with the crew copilot, Capt. Clevenger, and he said that would not be a problem. I guess I passed the "test," for I was transferred to Crew S26 the next day.

The crew flew twice before going to Tampa. I had several suggestions to make, but kept my mouth shut and did my job. They were well-coordinated and worked well together (not a surprise in as much as they had been together for more than three years). I received no instruction from anyone, much to my surprise. MSgt. Fritz gave me some suggestions. As the flight engineer, he knew what the score was, but was not overbearing. We were on our way to SES.

Prior to our flight evaluation flight, the crew lined up in front of the aircraft with parachutes and personal professional gear on display. The evaluator (a pilot) briefly questioned each crew member (I found out later he had tested this crew before). When he came to me, he immediately noticed my pilot wings sewn on my flight suit and looked me straight in the eye and said, "What the hell are you doing here?" I leaned forward, glancing at the aircraft commander (who looked like he was about to have a heart attack) and said "I am an AOB and my crew position is bombardier." He said no more to me and concentrated on the other members of the crew.

Two flights and ground testing later, we were to make simulated bomb runs over Phoenix and this was to be the most critical flight of all. I was to make two runs, different visual targets, followed by two radar runs by the radar operator. I made my two runs to be scored by the Radar Bomb Score (RBS) unit on the ground at Phoenix that was to be recorded by SAC. Normally, after a "bombs away," they gave you the score within five minutes. This time, however, there was a 15 minute delay in receiving my scores. The pilot asked me how I did and I responded,

"OK." He called the RBS site and asked them why the delay. The evaluator had no expression on his face, but was taking notes. He sat behind the pilot and copilot. They responded, "We have both of your scores. Both are the same. (In code) Both are direct hits. Do you copy?" That meant a "Pickle Barrel" award and the pilot, usually a very unemotional person let out a "whoop" that meant only one thing. I had held up my part. As far as visual bombing was concerned, the spot promotions were safe. The evaluator, now standing behind the pilot, said nothing and just shook his head, making a note.

The radar runs were fair, but within the allowable limits. We headed home to Tampa, but the number two engine failed and we had to land at Carswell AFB, Fort Worth, Texas a SAC base that had B-29s and B-36s. The rule in SAC, is that when operating under emergency conditions (including loss of one engine) the crew had to land at the nearest SAC base, if at all possible. We spent the next two days doing nothing but eating, sleeping and visiting the Base Exchange and Officers Club (in the evening). SAC sent us a Pratt and Whitney 3350 engine and the base maintenance section removed the failed engine and installed the new engine under the inquisitive supervision of Sgt. Fritz, our flight engineer. He knew his job better than any non-commissioned officer I worked with. We flight tested the aircraft and were back in business. The pilot got permission to fly back to Travis, having no further evaluations needed. I didn't ask, or care, how the evaluator got back to Tampa.

When we returned to Travis, the wing commander threw a party, at which time I was given the "Pickle Barrel" trophy for my accomplishments during the SES flight evaluation over Phoenix. It was an inscribed brass barrel, about three inches high on an oak base and a brass plate with my name on it. It was very special, particularly because it had never been awarded before in the Bomb Wing, but remained a SAC institution for years.

Chapter 4

OVERSEAS ROTATION

Our crew flew several training flights from early April to September, but nothing of consequence. We were to go overseas to Guam and Japan. I got several flights in the T-7, T-11 and C-47 as I knew I had to keep my hand in as a pilot. The B-29 is a good aircraft, but didn't give me the continued experience that a small aircraft can give you, especially in weather conditions.

The squadron started its rotation on September 15, flying during daylight to Hickam AFB, Hawaii. We landed ahead of four other B-29s from our squadron. The other 10 would arrive the next two days. We spent the night touring the city of Honolulu and took off on a test flight the next day. We had a rough-running engine. The spark plugs had fouled and had to be replaced. We were ready to go September 17, 1952 but were held up for some inexplicable reason. I never was told.

We took off the night of the 16th. It was agreed I would fly as navigator to Kwajalein Naval Air Station, about 3,600 miles from Hickam, all over water. I had planned the celestial mission and it went like clockwork. We landed 10-1/2 hours later without incident. The next leg was 6-1/2 hours and we landed at Anderson AFB, Guam the next day. When we gathered our gear and departed the plane (B-29MR No. 44-87767) the immediate weather was overpowering heat, almost taking the breath away. The temperature was about 100 degrees. To say it was hot would be a major understatement. Within five minutes our flying suits were soaked with sweat. The biggest problem was the humidity (amount of water in the air). Guam was an island in the midst of the Pacific Ocean and there was no relief from the humid climate.

We were herded into an open truck and started towards the billeting area when we heard B-29 engines revving up to maximum. Looking towards the runway, we saw a B-29 lumbering and accelerating slowly towards take-off. It looked like it was slow, as it was approaching the end of the runway. One hundred yards from the take-off was a cliff with a 100 foot drop to the open sea.

The B-29 finally raised its nose to take-off altitude and slowly lifted off within 50 feet of the end. After take-off the plane started to raise its landing gear, settled in a downward position and disappeared from view. The liaison officer made an off-hand comment, "Normal take-off for a weather ship with a full load." Greenwald nodded. What a revelation!

The next day the liaison officer group invited us to a luau, an outdoor party on the beach. The natives were experts at cooking pigs and we were impressed. The food was excellent and the party went on most of the night. The roasted pig was delicious. The fruit was excellent and the local drink packed a real wallop. It was a good indoctrination, but the heat, even at night was very disconcerting. A hangover followed the next morning.

We were given many weather briefings as well as a political explanation of Guamanian Culture that was very interesting. Guam is about 40 miles long and 10 miles wide. Agana is the capital city and the population at the time was more than 100,000. It is United States territory and its people are United States citizens. The island is the southernmost island of the Marianas chain, about 1,500 miles from the Philippines. The US Navy had a large base near Agana and a large shipping area on the southern end of the island. The main transportation was by motor scooter. Each crew had two scooters at their disposal. There were weekly trips to the Navy Exchange that was overstocked and much more expansive than that of what we were used to. There was no base exchange on the Guam Air Force Base. The language of the Guamanians was English. They were small in stature and very industrious. Their history is a polyglot. The Spaniards arrived in the 1500s and Japan took over the island in December 1941. The United States forces freed the people and island in August 1944.

We spent the first week acting like tourists. Our scooter was well-used and a welcome relief from the heat. Our quarters were tin-roofed, wooden sides with large windows and screens. Each had a "hot box," that we found out was a must because of the humidity. The "box" was four feet wide, five feet high and four feet deep. It was closed on the sides and back with plywood and the top was open with chicken wire. The front was closed with a hinged door. There was a hanger rod across the top and a shelf on the top and bottom. There was an electric light bulb behind the shoe rack that was illuminated 24 hours a day. In this climate, any clothes and especially the shoes, would get mold in a short time and literally destroy anything that was wet, or even damp (sweat, or damp ground). There was a lot of rain on the island. The light bulb generated the heat that was needed to stop the mold. Simple, but effective. The first thing that was checked in the morning was to make sure the bulb had not burned out.

We were scheduled to fly an over-water long distance flight of about 2,700 miles with small islands to be used as turning points and return to Anderson. Gunnery was part of the mission. Our radar operator had to be sure there were not any boats in the area before we could fire the tail guns. All the guns and turrets had been removed from the aircraft, except the tail guns, .50 caliber; this was done to give the aircraft more speed and this version of the B-29 was designated the B-29MR. The flight was in daylight so our navigator was using the sun as a reference so the accuracy of our location was not exact, but it was good training. Day missions were called PLOP (Planned Line of Position) and was based on using the sextant to line up our position, coupled with altitude and airspeed, would give us a fairly accurate location. Over water, without any landmarks, this was very valuable, but not as accurate as a form of navigation that the Weather Reconnaissance B-29s used, as I was to find out.

The flight was uneventful. The weather was clear and the winds were light and variable. It would have gotten boring, but I was using the sextant and Art Williams was doing the plotting. After the second leg, we switched positions. Our landfall at Guam was pretty good. We were five miles off and our estimated time of arrival was three minutes off. We were all satisfied. Six hours at 25,000 feet was pleasurable. I got to fly the "bird" part of the way.

On October 14, another AOB and I were called to the CO's office. We were escorted into his office by his secretary. The "boss" was at his desk and returned our salutes, casually. He asked if we wanted coffee (his office was air conditioned) and I immediately said "Yes," as did Lt. Nangle (who was the other AOB from a combat ready crew in the squadron). Before the coffee arrived he addressed me and asked if we were satisfied being "relegated" to a non-pilot status. Nangle said he was happy flying and I added "I'm getting pilot time with my crew and that helps." Holsey looked me in the eye and said, "You at least got the 'Pork Barrel'." I almost told him that award didn't help get me into the B-47 program, but I figured it was time to keep my mouth shut (one of the rare times I did).

Holsey pushed himself away from his desk and said in a very soft voice, "The 54th WRS is a good outfit and the CO is a good friend of mine. He is hurting for navigators and wants to borrow from us for one mission. What do you think?" We both knew we were being asked to fly with another command, but we knew the practice would be worth the effort and said "Yes." (What option did we have? We didn't volunteer, technically.) The CO smiled, then said we would be flying with the 54th Squadron CO and then asked if we had any LORAN experience. I answered for both of us. "Yes, we had practice for several hours on the ground simulator. I'm sure we could become familiar with the units in the aircraft if we could have instruction from the squadron navigator." (LORAN is Long Range Aid to Navigation).

LORAN is provided to the navigator and gave him a screen that showed radar pulses that could be identified by frequency and the navigator could pinpoint his position using special charts, not available to SAC. LORAN was used extensively in the Pacific area due to the vast stretches of water where landmarks were absent. It took two stations (channels) to obtain a "fix." These stations were spread all over the Pacific and transmitted their own individual pulses (each different) automatically.

The CO said we would get an update from the Weather Squadrons navigator on a WB-29 this afternoon (he surely must have believed we would accept his "offer." With the temperature close to 100 degrees this would be a real workout, but the two of us didn't have any choice.

After lunch we got a scooter and rode tandem to the WB-29 (No. 44-31709) and the first thing I noticed was all of the guns had been removed and there were several antennas protruding from the top of the fuselage. Surprise! There was a ground unit air conditioner pumping cold air into the crew compartment. The squadron navigator, Maj. Bishop was waiting for us near the escape hatch. Capt. Schwantz, the squadron weather officer, led us into the navigation compartment going through the weather equipment.

The navigators table was the same configuration as our SAC B-29s, except LORAN set was located above the indicators such as the altimeter, airspeed, temperature (outside air) and heading indicator. All standard. The navigator explained how the LORAN worked and how to use the special charts that went along with the set. He said I would be the chief navigator and Nangle would assist me. This was because I was a captain and he was a first lieutenant. Protocol in the strangest of places. One last thing, he showed us how to replace the set with another. Then he said it was important for there was a high rate of failure. He had us practice on the LORAN set, plotting and simulated removal of a "defective" set. While at Radar School at Mather AFB, we had simulator practice but couldn't practice in the air.

On October 19, we reported to the 54th briefing room at 0930 and were given the route and was told a typhoon may be building and we were to locate it and have the radar take pictures. We were to fly at 25,000 feet and if we found a typhoon were to fly over it, then fly through it at 10,000 feet, then fly through it at 500 feet. This sounded as exciting as cleaning your room at home.

We headed for a spot 750 miles northeast of Guam and then we saw ominous clouds up to 29,000 feet. The weather people took soundings. Nangle and I got so many LORAN fixes we lost count. It was rough flying at 25,000 feet. When we descended to 10,000 feet, we strapped in and held onto the navigators table. The thermals really were building up and the plane was up and down. I glanced at the two pilots. They were both on the controls. Finally, we descended to 500 feet and reversed our course. It was a flight to remember. The WB-29 was flopping all over the sky and you could see the choppy seas below. I only looked out of the navigator's window once. That was enough for me. I kept getting LORAN fixes to keep my mind occupied.

After what seemed an eternity the pilot, Col. Stephenson said it was time to go home and to give him a heading. I told him 200 degrees, that was a rough estimate. After a fast calculation, I added that the ETA was two hours and 15 minutes later. My estimate was to be fairly accurate. LORAN is a great navigation tool. I wish SAC had it.

Finally, the radar operator spoke up and said that Guam was 10 degrees right at 90 miles. The pilot turned to the new heading and started a slow descent (we had climbed back to 26,000 feet) and approached Anderson. After the flight was over and we were leaving the aircraft, Col. Stephenson thanked us for the "excellent job" we did. Our squadron CO was there and happy to see his people were safe. We got a pat on the back from him. Flight time: 10 hours and 50 minutes.

After an extensive debriefing, I collected my thoughts and realized that with the proper training any air crew member could do any job and I surmised that was the background decision to convert a nine-member crew combat ready group to a three-man crew with more capability. Every SAC AOB on Guam was scheduled to fly with the 54th, because of our capability we demonstrated on the initial flight. It helped that the squadron commander was the chief pilot. This weather squadron was sadly lacking in navigators. Why I don't know. Priorities, would be my guess.

Suddenly, after two flights with the weather squadron, the remainder of the AOB supporting flights were canceled with no explanation. Being "experts," we were in demand and on display and briefed several groups on what to expect, all for naught, fortunately. We were not trained for this type flying, but I personally enjoyed the special navigation. Good experience and it added to our confidence. The reason for SAC AOBs not flying with weather squadron was revealed to us when we got back to Travis in December 1952. The SAC AOB project was the brainchild of Gen. Curtis LeMay and he followed its progress very closely. He found out we were flying with another command's aircraft and almost had a heart attack (figuratively), according to some friends of mine. He personally issued a direct order to each unit who had AOBs that "they" were not to be used for any non-SAC activity. He fired the squadron commanders and the 9th Bomb Wing commander. I flew for Gen. LeMay in 1944 (8th Air Force England) and knew of his ruthless approach to projects he had put forth. He accepted no irresponsible or counter-productive activities.

Chapter 5

ROTATION RETURN

The squadron was nearing its rotation date and feelings were running high. The base commander gave us a "going away" luau party on the beach at Anderson. The talk of the party was the fact that two AOBs "found" the typhoon and we were kept busy answering questions about how it felt and what happened "in" the typhoon (the same as a hurricane, except the wind was in the opposite direction in the southern hemisphere). Were we impressed by LORAN? We were even asked how it was flying with another command (they were more loose and not so much following the strictness we were used to in SAC). Were we impressed by LORAN as a principal means of navigation (yes)? Bill Greenwald, never an emotional pilot, came up to me during the later part of the party, put his arm around my shoulder and said he was going to miss me, knowing my time was limited with my going to the B-47 program soon. Art Williams, our navigator from Texas, sat down beside me on a fallen coconut tree and thanked me for helping him. With that having been said, he moved toward the bar saying he needed a drink (he had several already).

As I was nursing my rum punch, our radar operator, Allie Mussey staggered up and with his face right up to mine, said he was proud of me and wished me the best of luck. He weaved off towards the bar. I found out the next day he had wandered off and passed out. No one noted he was absent until early the next day. Greenwald got the non-coms and they went to the beach and ultimately found him, snuggled up under a pile of palm leaves. Thank goodness he didn't try to take a swim. They dragged him into a jeep and drove him back to our quarters and put him to bed, still in his clothes. They tried to wake him, but he never woke and slept the whole day!

The next two days were spent sleeping, eating and visits to the Navy exchange. We were trying to pick up gifts for those back home. Being a bachelor, my gift list was smaller than most. I was satisfied with getting my liquor allowance to bring back. For most of the crew (Radar was the biggest purchaser, he had to go in a jeep instead of the motor scooter). The NCOs had a lot of "friends," back at Travis and got more than their share.

Our return would be the reverse of coming out to Guam. Naval Air Station Kwajalein was first, then to Hickam where we would have to go through customs, then the final leg to Travis. We were to leave Guam on December 16 and land at Travis on the 19th if all things went well and the weather was in our favor. Preparations were made. We loaded our plane (44-87767), with the flight engineer MSgt. Fritz changing the spark plugs on all four engines and checking the instruments. He did not want anything to go wrong. He was ready to go home. On the day before we were to take-off, I took all my gear and loaded my footlocker in the forward bomb bay where a wooden rack was supported from the bomb shackles, thanks to Sgt. Fritz I might add. I noticed when I entered the aft section of the radar compartment, I heard someone moving around the back of the aircraft. I noted the plexiglas blisters were open on both sides of the fuselage. As I moved forward, I noticed the access door to the aft bomb bay was open, allowing entrance to the collapsible fuel tank we always carried on our flights, although it was always empty. The tank, when full, carried 2,000 gallons of fuel. The tank had vent holes on the outside of the fuselage to allow fumes to dissipate, thus reducing the possibility of fire.

With the aft bomb bay door open there was a two foot by three foot access panel to the tank. It was open and that was peculiar. Then I saw a head coming through the panel, followed by the rest of the body. It was TSgt. Robert Conzet, the tail gunner and refueling operator. He was five feet two inches and weighed about 100 pounds and was the only man able to manhandle his way into the empty bomb bay tank. He smiled and waved. The look on my face made him smile even more. He motioned me to come and take a look in the tank. He handed me a flashlight. I peered into the cavity and was surprised to see about 10 cases of whiskey, stacked on a series of wooden slats and tied down. He said this was standard procedure and since he was on his third rotation, it must have been safe. Nothing more needed to be said. He slapped me on the back and proceeded to put the access panel in place and screwed down the bottles. Then he sealed the plate in place and that was that. Crew integrity, none of my business.

We took off at dusk on December 16, landed on Kwajalein, went through refueling and finally landed at Hickam 10 hours later at about 5:00 p.m. We were subjected to customs search on the ramp in front of our aircraft. Some 45 minutes later, the three civilians gave us their clearance and we were on our way to our hotel in Honolulu.

Two days later we spent enough time to be classified as tourists walking around downtown. The restaurants got our undivided attention, as did the fruit bars. The fresh pineapple, mangoes and bananas caused a certain amount of discomfort, but it was worth it. Other than getting two of the crew out of the police detention barracks (for an "argument" with several naval types) as a gesture of international good will, the "rest and recuperation" was a success. We reloaded our B-29 and prepared for the final leg home.

At the appointed time on December 19, all of the crews met at Base Operations and filed our flight plans. It would take about six hours and we had plenty of fuel, for the weather at Travis was a low overcast with rain. It didn't cross my mind that we would have trouble landing.

About an hour from the mainland, we saw the weather along the coast. We had taken off 15 minutes apart, the first was the CO at 8:15 a.m. We were second, Berodt third and so on. All 10 took off without incident. We were cruising at 25,000 feet and were already under verbal contact with San Francisco Center. The lead aircraft was already at 10,000 feet, 20 miles from Travis. We were cleared to 10,000 feet and started our descent. Then we were cleared to 4,000 feet. Travis weather was 400 feet overcast, two miles in rain and we were then cleared for our approach. Greenwald was an old hand at this and I saw the runway through the layers of clouds. The rain was very heavy, but we landed without much trouble. After touchdown the water spewed on both sides of the wings helping us to slow down. We were back and I, for one, was happy to be back to my quarters and cooler weather.

The wing commander met each aircraft and we unloaded our gear into a covered truck to be taken to our squadron flight-line offices and lockers. We got wet, especially when I got my footlocker out of the bomb bay with the help of the crew. The rain didn't bother us. We were just glad to be home. After we had stowed our gear and were waiting for the bus to take us to our quarters, Sgt. Fritz came up to me and said in hushed tones, "Are you staying here?" I said that I was going to San Francisco to spend some time with my folks. He smiled, leaned closer and said, "Well, if you get back early, stop by my place in Fairfield. We're going to have a party that will last a week." He winked and left, his girlfriend was waiting for him outside.

We had nothing to do until the Christmas party on December 24. The festivities were somewhat subdued, except for a few altercations in the early morning, but the partygoers were pretty well controlled and by breakfast at 5:00 a.m. no one went home and we all had a community breakfast. I struggled back to my room and collapsed on the bed. I slept through the day and night and finally awakened the next morning, feeling like I was in a car wreck. I struggled into the shower and spent the next 30 minutes enjoying the hot water. I began to feel human again.

After getting dressed, I packed a couple changes of clothes and got into my two-door Packard, hoping it would start. I had made arrangements for one of my friends to drive the car and fill it up with gas before I got back.

The "Green Hornet" started the first time and I patted the dashboard and wheeled out of the parking lot heading for San Francisco to spend a few days with my mother. I stopped off at a restaurant in Vallejo, ate a hearty breakfast and headed for "the city."

The drive across the bay bridge brought back many thoughts of an earlier time. The sight was a welcome one. The skyline of San Francisco never failed to bring a smile to my face. The visit with my mother was a pleasurable one. We talked of my escapades on Guam and she told of her opening a new school for the gifted, the first one in northern California. She visited with the governor and thought he was a good, gentle man. The next days went by fast, we ate twice at Fisherman's Wharf (the prices were even higher than I remembered) and then at LeBoeufs in the financial district. We had a glorious time. I hated to leave, but I was secretly looking forward to getting back into flying and the thought of the B-47 program, that had to be shortly, I kept telling myself. My mother was very interested in when and where I was going next. Unfortunately, I had no answers. She got me to promise I'd let her know the minute I found out.

The drive back was a long one. It was December 30 and I wanted to get back in time for the New Year's party. When I got back to the base, there was no flying activity going on. I called the pilot and confirmed there was no transfer orders for me and he was looking forward to the party the next evening. He chuckled and told me he had a secret he'd tell me about at the party. I thanked him and wondered what was going on. I unpacked my gear and went down to a community washer and dryer. There was no one there. Most of the bachelors were home for the holidays.

The next morning I got up and went to the Officers Club for breakfast. Afterwards, I drove down to squadron operations and checked in with the duty officer (in SAC, each combat squadron had an officer on duty 24 hours). There was no news, except he told me I was scheduled to fly with a new crew January 6, then ferry a B-29 war weary bird to the Aberdeen Proving Grounds, Maryland, so the field artillery could practice shooting at it on the ground. There was no schedule after that. I drove to Base Operations (they were open 24-hours a day to handle any incoming and outgoing airplane traffic).

The Base Operations officer was in his office, so I dropped in and we talked. He was planning the February flight schedule and I asked to be scheduled for a lot of flights. He agreed and gave me a flight schedule that included three flights in a C-45 and six in a T-11. I was happy to keep busy. My B-29 crew was on leave during January and that meant I could do what I wanted. Very good.

The secret the pilot wanted to tell me was that a group of our squadron pilots decided that our CO needed some "action" and planned to take his car, a yellow Morris Minor (English) and put it on the flat roof of his quarters. The boss and his wife had to be at the Officers Club at 4:00 p.m. on New Year's Eve to supervise setting up the party. The base civil engineer was a good friend of Col. Holsey who had been promoted the day after we returned. He was in on the plan for he had to provide a mobile crane used primarily to move big aircraft engines. He had one of his sergeants (who we paid) park the crane around the corner from the quarters. He knew what the car looked like and when we saw the CO and his wife leave, he moved the crane behind the Morris. By this time the conspirators were hitching the car to the lift crane. The car was elevated high enough to get on the flat roof, maneuvering the crane. Once the car was on the right roof (all housing was one story high), one of the men climbed onto the roof by way of a ladder and unhitched the shackles. Everyone left, including the crane and operator. It took 15 minutes and everything was back to "normal." The "Old Man" missed his car when he came home. No one said anything at the party and he almost went crazy until he saw the car the next day and that really made him wild. He never did find out who did such a "dastardly" trick on him, but I think he had a good idea the civil engineer was in on it. For he knew the CE would be the one who could provide what was needed.

Being by myself was fine. I flew seven times in January and four times in February; including a ferry flight to Herrington, Kansas to deliver a T-11 for storage. This trip was right up my alley. We would take-off on Friday and deliver the aircraft on Monday, the scheduled date.

The Beechcraft T-11 twin engine training aircraft had twin Pratt & Whitney 450 horsepower engines. It had range of 3-1/2 hours. We took off early Friday, landing at Victorville, CA; El Paso, Texas; Big Springs, Texas and stopped at Dallas, Texas for the weekend. Dallas is a great city and it was a good place to have a nice time. We took off Monday morning and landed at Herrington, Kansas by noon.

When we returned (by commercial air), everything was normal. I checked in at the squadron and to my surprise, my orders had come through. I was transferred to Lake Charles AFB in southwestern Louisiana, no later than March 7, 1953. My orders had me assigned as a copilot and listed my pilot as a Capt. Gene Peirson, who was currently stationed at Davis-Monthan AFB, Tucson, AZ. I knew nothing about him, he knew nothing about me. That made us even.

Chapter 6

INTRODUCTION TO THE B-47

There were three of us transferred from Travis to Lake Charles to be copilots. We got together and decided to use one of the cars, a Buick four-door, and the others would sell their cars. I was glad to get rid of the Packard. It passed everything on the road except a gas station, 9.6 miles to the gallon. It was eating me up. There was plenty of room for all of our gear and we would each drive two hours and split the costs. We left on February 28 and pulled into Lake Charles March 1. We signed in at Wing Headquarters and I was assigned to the 67th Bomb Squadron. The other two were assigned to the 66th Bomb Squadron. We all decided to find a house near the base and went house-hunting immediately. As luck would have it, we found a little two bedroom place outside the west gate; two baths and it had lots of room for storage. The rent was a bit steep, but three of us could handle it.

I talked to the squadron operations officer, a Maj. Ruben Nye (a B-29 pilot) and he had my flight records. He said I needed an instrument card check before I left for Pinecastle (Orlando, Florida) for B-47 upgrading. I was scheduled to check (required annually) with Capt. Bill Buckland on March 4, 1953 in a B-29 and he was to get his instrument check on the same flight.

The flight was flown on schedule and both of us passed. We didn't get to demonstrate everything on the checklist for the weather was marginal, at best, but everything went smoothly and that took care of a requirement for me. I didn't realize all B-47 upgrades had to have a current instrument card and the squadron was not about to send one of its pilots needing one. After a debriefing by Buckland, he told me to wait for him a few minutes. Nye came in shortly thereafter with a small thin captain in his flying suit. He introduced me to Gene Peirson. he smiled and gave me a firm handshake. The major left and Peirson and I were left alone. He said we were leaving by Douglas C-47 on March 21. I told him we had a small rented house, and he said he had to leave and that his wife was out house-hunting.

B-47E 51-2395, over northern Georgia. Note lack of wing tanks. They were installed during a modification cycle, at the Lockheed, Marietta, Georgia, facility.

On March 21, we climbed aboard the C-47 and were on our way to Pinecastle. Along with Peirson and me, there was Max Judas, Al Bissonnette and Bob Sprankle. I didn't know any of them, but it was obvious they knew Peirson. They talked pilot talk, so Sprankle and I looked and were bored. The five hour flight was spent drinking coffee and sleeping for the most part. After landing we were shepherded to the transient student quarters. We were together in the same building. Then we went down to Training Operations and were briefed along with about 50 more students on our flight schedule in the Lockheed T-33, a two-seat jet single engine trainer. The next two days were spent learning the systems of the T-33 and on March 24, I got my first flight. I completed the training on April 16 and couldn't get the right main gear down, so had to use the emergency hydraulic system to get it extended and locked. What a way to end the first part of our training.

The first phase of our T-33 training was one-day ground training and one-day flying. It took 30 days and we were ready, theoretically for the B-47. On April 27, 1953 Peirson and I, with our instructor Lt. Oliver flew our first flight in the TB-47B (50-069), an early model of the Stratojet. Basically it was like the same we would fly back home, except our B-47E would have improved fuel system and the latest radar set.

I spent our first flight (four hours and 20 minutes) sitting below and to the left of the copilots seat (called the fourth man position) and read the checklist when asked for. I closely watched the instructor and what he did so I could emulate him when I got in the rear seat.

We flew six more flights and I finally got in the back seat. On our seventh flight was May 7 and it was interesting. The only real concern was that I was sitting on an ejection seat (the fourth position had no ejection seat). By this time I was used to the checklist and where everything was. I got to actually fly the "bird" for three minutes. It was something to be on the controls.

It was sensitive on the controls and I used the trim tabs extensively (I learned that while flying on the Berlin Air Lift in 1949). At the debriefing the IP commented on my use of trim. It was his experience most new pilots tried to "muscle" the B-47. I found out early that it was too tiring. When flying for six to eight hours, you use what you can and thus reducing the fatigue and stress.

We flew our check flight on May 19 and flew a solo flight on May 29. We had a good time. The flight was uneventful, but Peirson commented that he felt we were "pushed" through the training program. I didn't disagree with him, but I got the feeling that SAC wanted its pilots in a hurry. I was surprised and dejected because we learned nothing about air refueling. A job I was really looking forward to, but I guessed I'd take it slow, learn what I could and keep my patience under control.

Chapter 7

COMBAT CREW TRAINING (MOROCCO)

When we got back to Lake Charles, I spent most of my time talking to crew members who had not been through Pinecastle yet, as one who was the first, it was somewhat of an oddity. During the first week in June, a cadre of instructor pilots arrived from MacDill (the 305th and 306th BW) had been flying the B-47B for about six months and were sent to the units who were about to get the new planes. On June 24, I was scheduled to copilot with Capt. Hugh Gregory (an IP) to go to Boeing-Wichita and pick up our new B-47E. On June 25, we picked up B-47E (51-5237) and flew it back with a flight time of two hours. Gregory let me make the approach and first landing from the back seat and that was exciting. The copilot, if looking straight ahead, is looking at the back of the ejection seat of the pilot, so he has to lean against the right canopy to land. It's not as easy as it sounds. The landing was fair with Gregory coaching me so I wouldn't land nosewheel first.

The next time I was scheduled for an aircraft pickup was July 29. When the pilot, Capt. Ray Green and I landed we were told our aircraft was not ready. It had an engine problem, but it would be ready the next day. That meant a night on the town. Green had been in Wichita before and knew his way around. We had a good time and I didn't drink very much for we had to fly the next day. The next morning, July 1, our new plane was ready (51-5225) and we had no problem on the trip back. Green had something to do, so we landed after only one hour and 35 minutes of flight.

Our crew was filled when we were assigned Capt. Ray Watson. I don't know whether or not Peirson hand-picked him or took who Wing Operations gave us. We had a lot to accomplish, so our flight planning was detailed. Peirson didn't like making the radio calls and I enjoyed that part of any flight. Reading the checklist was important, but timing was what made a crew cohesive. Ray flight planned and I made up my own flight plan for timing and fuel consumption.

As we rolled onto the runway, Peirson increased power on all six engines. "Tower, Blast 32, ready for take-off." We were cleared and started our take-off roll. As we accelerated, I checked the engine performance and then called our airspeed. "110, rotate at 130." Peirson pulled back on the yoke and we were off the ground, still accelerating. As we passed 500 feet and 260 knots, the number one engine exhaust gas temperature (EGT) was getting too hot. I retarded the left engine, told Peirson we could lose No. 1 and he confirmed my reading. Bringing back the throttle didn't stabilize the engine temperature and I told Peirson we ought to shut the engine down. I looked to the left and there was no sign of fire. He put the engine in cutoff and said to notify Control and the tower we were returning to the base. I switched to tower frequency and told them we were going to stay in the local area, advising them we had lost an engine, but not declaring an emergency at this time. The tower responded and told us to keep them advised. I switched to Control frequency.

"Blast Control, this is Blast 32. We have a problem, over."

"Blast 32, Control. What is your problem, over."

"Control 32. Lost No. 1 engine, high EGT and staying in the local area. Will advise any further complications, over."

"32, Blast Control. Roger. Do you need assistance, over?"

"Control, 32. Not at this time, but alert Chase to standby."

Peirson broke in. "Dave, want to fly for awhile?" I told him I had the aircraft and headed for Galveston at 10,000 feet. No particular reason. It was pretty down there from the air.

Once over the city, I looked to the right, saw Houston, hazy in the distance and Ellington AFB. I turned left, out over the Gulf away from any traffic and headed back towards the base.

Peirson said we should call Spector Control and ask them if they wanted to calibrate their ground radar. The continental Air Command operated radar sets all over the United States, a network of long distance radar sets. Its purpose was to monitor aircraft and directing fighter aircraft onto unidentified aircraft, assisting aircraft with emergencies and assisting crews to a suitable landing site. There was a new site south of our base, but very few of our pilots used their facility.

I switched to GCI (Ground Control Intercept) frequency. "Spector Control, this is Blast 32, over." They responded immediately.

"Blast 32, this is Spector. How may we be of assistance? Over."

"Spector, Blast 32. Will be in the local area for two hours. Can we be of assistance in your calibration?" There was a long silence. Apparently they had a lot of trouble aligning their radar on aircraft. We played with them for about an hour, going from Lake Charles to New Orleans, to Shreveport to Houston and in between. It was very interesting and helped us pass the time profitably.

Once airborne, we were committed to three hours of flight time before we could get the aircraft reduced in weight to an acceptable limit. It was a critical landing weight (125,00 pounds) because of landing gear limit and landing distance.

The next year we flew crew missions, special operations and went on Wing sorties to Loring AFB, ME, landing in a snow storm. That was exciting. Most of flight time the Wing was in the throes of upgrading new observers and our crew missions were few and far between. I spent almost all of my time checking out copilots. The Wing had appointed me as the operations officer for Chase Operations. The copilots had to learn chase techniques. We had a requirement to have a qualified pilot on standby, each of the three squadrons provided pilots for the purpose of flying formation with a B-47 that had a faulty airspeed problem (that was a periodic problem throughout SAC). The airspeed on final approach of the B-47E was five knots above stall speed (based on aircraft weight so the accurate airspeed reading was essential). Throughout SAC there were B-47E airspeed problems, so each unit was assigned six T-33s to fly "chase" and would compare airspeed with the bomber in the traffic area, including the final approach and landing (that was the tricky part). If a call would come from the B-47 notifying of an airspeed problem, the T-33 pilot on standby in his ready room would get to the T-33 and take-off. They were given priority and very soon were in sight of the "stricken bird" and quickly slid into formation on the right of the B-47 and made radio contact and called off speeds, to verify the bombers speed indications and asked what he wanted to "hold (air speed)." Especially, I wanted to know what his final approach speed was. It was a lot of fun for the T-33, but the B-37 was hoping they could get the "monster" on the ground safely.

Peirson and I talked a lot about flying and he asked me if flying the C-54 on the airlift was as monotonous as he was given to understand. I told him, in rather a loud voice, that, that kind of flying was the best instrument flying anyone could obtain. It was a thrill for me and I would do it again if the necessity arose. He smiled and said I was ready to move into the front seat (no one had done so in the Wing). Before I could respond he said he thought I was wasting my time in the back seat, indicating I would be the first copilot to be upgraded to aircraft commander. My face betrayed my feelings and I said he wouldn't be sorry to nominate me. He patted me on the back and said he would get the ball rolling. I found out later he had talked to Maj. Jack Chartier, our flight commander. He was a B-47 pilot for three years, coming from MacDill. Jack and I were friends and he said he was impressed with the way I had set up the T-33 program. Jack said I was the logical copilot to move up. He became my instructor. We started the upgrading on March 3, 1954. Jack was a great instructor, letting you almost make a mistake before he corrected, helped more than most of the instructors who generally yelled at you long before they had to.

The instruction was coming along nicely. We spent most of the first three flights practicing instrument approaches. The B-47 was an excellent instrument flying machine and easy to control. After flying 185 trips on the Berlin Air Lift in 1949, I felt at ease using radar and instrumentation to make approaches. Landing the bicycle-gear B-47 was a flat-type approach, almost in the landing position before you came over the end of the runway. The only thing to consider was not to land nose first because the "bird" would bounce back in the air and that was a dangerous position. The best way to land a B-47 was to touchdown aft wheels first, retard the throttles and lower the forward gear smoothly. That comes with practice and Jack was very tolerant if I goofed the landing.

I finished my upgrading check on March 27 and my inflight refueling on March 28 over Fort Myers, Florida (we had to take a tanker wherever we could). I had made the grade and took over a crew whose pilot had failed his standardization check and was relegated to a copilots position. SAC could be very unforgiving. I was concerned that his crew was somewhat responsible for the pilot's failure, but prejudging was something none of us wanted to get into. I knew I was "on trial" with the copilot and navigator, but that was their problem, not mine.

The next days went quickly. We were alerted for an overseas rotation April 17, 1954, just 20 days after I had passed my flight check. No time for the weak. Preparation for the deployment (called Daily Double) took the better part of a week. Packing summer clothes, flying gear and a hundred other things, including a camera and lots of film, took time. Also, we had to plan the flight, and having a new copilot and navigator who had flown one time together wasn't the easiest thing to do without having become accustomed to each other. Oliver Boynton was the copilot and Russ Hempel was the radar/navigator. Both were qualified. Our crew was R46A0, so I shouldn't have many major problems and I told them so. They seemed to understand the pilot I had replaced was not my idea, so we should get along.

Russ flight planned, as did I, and Oliver checked the aircraft (51-5240) a hundred times. No. 240 was assigned to our crew. I had flown it before and it was a good plane to fly. The radar was reliable and had not been flown until the deployment date.

The day before the rotation, we briefed on our mission profile. The 66th Squadron was to take-off at 0800 with five aircraft, the 67th would follow at 0900. Deacy would lead, Chartier was No. 2, I was No. 3, Jackson was No. 4 and Sullivan was No. 5. We would fly a loose formation at 33,000 feet and refuel east of Charleston, SC at 15,000 feet with an onload of 32,000 pounds (5,000 gallons). The 68th would leave at 10:00 a.m. with five aircraft. The reason for the hour delay was so that the tankers could rotate in and out of Savannah, Georgia in order that each flight could get enough fuel to get to Morocco. Our refueling squadron, the 44 AREFS, would take-off with 16 aircraft and land at Hunter AFB, Savannah three days before we would need them. Then they would land and prepare for their long flight supporting us. They would then spend their rotation at Nouasseur Air Base outside of Casablanca, a lot better than us. We would land at Sidi Slimane Air Base outside of Port Lyautey on the northwest coast of Morocco. In the desert we were to spend our 90 days.

The 66th had taken off at 0700 with perfect weather on April 17 and we were ready an hour later and took off without any problems. We turned on course, checked in with Blast Control climbing to 35,000 feet. Oliver said he had the first two aircraft above and ahead. Russ confirmed this by his radar. The leader announced he was at altitude and kept his speed at 220 knots until we got in loose formation and then he would increase speed to 240 knots. Each of us confirmed our location. We drew close to the lead aircraft and Russ announced we would reach descent point to air refueling at one hour and 40 minutes.

As we approached the descent point, Russ said he had the tanker's beacons (electronically) on his radar. He counted five beacons, so we all were going to be able to get fuel. At this point the leader said to "close it up" and started to descend at 280 knots and down we all went, staggered to the right. We stayed in formation with Russ calling off the distances until we leveled out at 14,500, four miles back. Deacy said the tankers were at 180 knots and if we had our tanker, to go on in and get our fuel on our own. By this time I had the five tankers in sight and lined up with their No. 3. I switched to my assigned radio frequency and called, "Storm 64, this Blast 43 coming in. Do you have me in sight?"

"Roger 3, this is No. 3 tanker, we have you in sight and we are ready. 32,000 pounds available."

The air refueling went well. The tanker maintained a good stable platform and we got all of the fuel we were authorized in one contact. Not bad.

"Receiver 3, this is tanker 3. You have your fuel. Disconnect on the count of three. 1-2-3, disconnect." We dropped below the tanker and accelerated. Oliver said we were well ahead of the other four B-47s, so we started our climb. The rest of the flight (10 hours and 30 minutes) was normal. We landed first and were met by the wing commander (he flew in the first 66th aircraft). He shook hands with each of us and then left to greet the other four, who had lined up for landing.

The overseas rotation was a slow one. We didn't fly much. Our main interest was dropping practice bombs from 25-30,000 feet at Ksar-Es-Souk Bombing Range on the eastern side of the Atlas Mountains. It was maintained by the French Foreign Legion. Besides that, John Deacy, Tex Jackson and I took a train to Tangier on the north tip of Morocco on the Mediterranean Ocean. We spent three days wandering around and trying to stay out of trouble in the Native Quarter. Our guide was an Arab and spoke good English.

Jackson's crew and mine got a five-day leave and flew our aircraft individually into RAF Fairford, near Norwich, England and had a good time in London. The flight back was uneventful. Breathing oxygen at 100 percent helped cure a mild hangover.

B-47E 52-3359, with SAC insignia. Note wing tanks (1,540 gallons each), that were standard equipment on all training flights. They were ejected when empty, if used during periods of conflict.

Chapter 8

Redeployment

The return deployment was scheduled to start June 14, 1954 with five aircraft from each squadron fitted with two 10,000 pound (1,562 gallon) wing tanks. The configuration was designed to expand the range of the B-47E in an Emergency War Order (EWO) situation and to be dropped when empty (about one hour and 15 minutes to transfer). The problem was it took four hours to install them and the "big boys" decided to keep them on the wings of the B-47 (the wing tanks were too expensive to drop after every flight). In other words, we had to haul them around on each flight. That cut down the range and initially increased the weight. That wasn't too bad but tests showed the reliability of the tanks to be "ejected" and the failure of the tanks to feed had happened too frequently. The crew could not empty one tank (if the other failed to transfer fuel to the main tanks) because the pilot could not trim the aircraft with one tank full (or partially full) and one tank empty. The engineers installed a rail system so that when the wing tanks were empty and released under wartime conditions, a nine foot parachute would be deployed (by a switch on the pilots console) causing the tanks to be pulled on the rails and released off of the B-47E. This mechanical release system didn't always work during the flight tests and the crews had little confidence in them. By design, the wing tank's other continuing problem was the tanks feeding to the engines through the main tanks. The wing tanks had no booster pumps relying on air pressure fed from the engines into the fuel lines. If both tanks fed properly, everything was fine. If neither tank fed, the crew would have to carry 20,000 pounds for an entire mission (we always transferred fuel first from them) and lose two hours of range and reduce the airspeed to keep the structural integrity because of the tank limitations. All in all, the wing tanks were a pain, but we learned to live with them. Each squadron had five aircraft fitted with wing tanks. The 15 (all three squadrons, intermixed) were to take-off at 30 minute intervals (between groups) and refuel southwest of Bermuda.

The tankers were staged out of Kindley AFB, Bermuda. They got all the breaks. When the first five B-47s (they had the tanks) took off, the aircraft required 8,500 feet of runway to take-off and at Sidi Slimane had 9,000 feet of runway. The temperature was the key. The B-47E was a "ground lover," the airplane would fly when it was ready and not before. The pilot couldn't pull it off the ground like other aircraft. A fact that had to be lived with. As the temperature reached 90 degrees Fahrenheit, take-off could be a big problem. We were to see this action shortly.

The first five (from the 66th) taxied out. The temperature was 87 degrees. They all took off at one minute intervals with not much runway remaining. A group of us were standing at the end and side of the strip. So far so good. The next squadron (68th) were starting their engines and shortly were taxiing and then down to the far of the runway. The temperature was 93 degrees and each airplane took off at about the 9,000 (last) runway marker. One aircraft, No. 5, used almost all of the runway. Wobbling to the air, it started to climb as it retracted the gear. Getting close to trouble. Our squadron was next.

The 67th was lined up and the temperature was 95 degrees. Above the safety limit, but they were going to go. After 90 days in Morocco, judgment was compromised so the crews could get home. I remember thinking, "I'm glad my bird didn't have wing tanks." Not too encouraging. Chartier was No. 1, Sullivan was No. 2, Bissonnette was No. 3, Starkey No. 4 and Mead, No. 5. As they taxiied, I noted Bissonnette (from Fresno, CA) had not started to taxi. About two minutes later he came out of the parking area going about twice as fast as the others trying to catch up with the other four. He just took over the last spot for there was no way to sandwich himself in his original No. 3 position.

The first four were airborne at 9,000 feet and all staggered into the air, but the take-off roll was getting critical. No. 5 brought his power up to maximum (100 percent) and started to accelerate. The temperature was 97 degrees and Bissonnette was halfway down the runway. With binoculars, I saw the landing gear struts had not lightened, that would have indicated lift was occurring.

This was going to be close. He was beyond the point where he could retard the throttles, deploy the chute and be able to stop before the end of the runway. He was committed. At the 9,000 foot marker he was still on the ground. When he passed the end of the runway, rocks flew in all directions, but he was in the air, barely. He kept the aircraft from trying to climb, about one minute later. I could see he had raised the nose, retracted the gear and slowly started to climb. He was one of the more experienced pilots in the Wing (he was the leading cadre going to Pinecastle with Peirson and me). I talked to him after we returned to Lake Charles and he said he had seen the end of the runway and pulled back on the yoke and the aircraft staggered into the air. He said he could feel the rocks hitting the underside of the wings, but kept the back pressure. He admitted he was lucky, but cursed the wing tanks, as did most of us.

We were told later in the day, Starkey could not get one wing tank to feed and had to return to Sidi Slimane. He landed three hours later, quite dejected. The maintenance people found a one-way float valve had failed to open. The tank was emptied and the valve repaired. Then the tank was filled and pressure was applied by a ground power unit and the new valve worked correctly. He was then schedule to fly with our squadron the next day.

The wing liaison officer made arrangements that the first tanker flight included six tankers to accommodate our six aircraft. That was not a problem, for the third flight of tankers would make up the difference, then recycle the one aircraft and make it up on the last flight. We were briefed on the afternoon of the June 15, flight planned, and checked the "Prowler" (my nickname for No. 240, our aircraft, although this was frowned upon by SAC), had an early dinner and went to bed. We had a 9:00 a.m. take-off and that meant we would have to have breakfast at 6:00 a.m.

By the time we got to the aircraft the heat was building, but not like yesterday, thank goodness. We were in our seats strapped in at 8:40 a.m. and got the engines started at 8:50 a.m. and fell in as No. 4. Starkey, with the wing tanks was No. 6. The first three got off on time and then it was our turn. We were cleared for take-off, temperature was 80 degrees. I moved the throttles to 100 percent and Oliver said all six were stabilized. I released the brakes and we were rolling, slowly.

"Go-No go speed, NOW. On the mark."

"Take-off speed in 10 ... NOW." The airplane was airborne at 8,500 feet and we were on our way. The gear and flaps were up and accelerating to 310 knots, climbing.

"I have the other three ahead, five miles and above," Russ stated. "5 and 6 are behind us to the right," Oliver said as we passed through 20,000 feet.

"On course, air refueling at 1410," Russ pitched in. We didn't need any navigation requirements, so we just "followed the leader," depending on the lead navigator to get us to the refueling area. Russ took a few sun lines that gave us our speed. Oliver practiced the radar gunnery using No. 6 as a target. By 1400 we were looking forward to taking on fuel. We were scheduled for a 40,000 pound (6,250 gallons) onload that took about 20 minutes, if we had a good contact. The descent was satisfactory, except we passed through some clouds at 20,000 feet and came into the clear at 16,000. Russ had picked the tanker beacons and was giving me heading and distances.

"Five miles, heading 260." We were to refuel at 16,000 feet. When we were out of the clouds, I saw the six tankers ahead and slightly above us.

The refueling was satisfactory. We onloaded 42,000 pounds (6,560 gallons). I had two disconnects, because of the turbulence. We were in good shape to get back to Lake Charles. We climbed to 33,000 feet and fell into loose information.

The arrival was no problem. The weather was good and we were cleared to land one after the other. We spaced ourselves making a visual approach. The 66th had already landed and we were met by the squadron staff. Because of SAC's policy of no civilians on the flight line, the wives, girlfriends and the children were waiting in front of our briefing room. Flight time was 11 hours and 35 minutes. We landed in front of the crowd with our gear aboard the truck. Went into our Operations building. Suddenly we were tired and felt like home. The words sounded good even though my quarters were going to be lonely. It was June 16, 1954.

A B-47E without wing tanks, refueling with a KC-97 tanker. Note the open IFR door. The white paint was not standard in SAC.

Chapter 9

THE PREPARATION

In the Strategic Air Command (known as SAC throughout the military) the test of each unit's effectiveness was measured by its capability to respond to and fly a Headquarters directed long-range mission against specified targets in any part of the world and return.

Headquarters SAC (located south of Omaha, NE) started the ball rolling by sending a message to a specific wing through its exclusive and extensive communications network by voice. It was then followed by a teletype message called a frag (for frag-mentation) order. The frag order outlines dates, times, routes, tar-gets, air refueling, recovery and destination procedures. The ba-sic timing had been pre-planned and supporting units were in-cluded in this order. Each crew of every operating wing, on a monthly basis, reviews the flight plans and updates them with current winds. Each navigator has at least four possible routes to contend with and he stays busy.

In the 1950s the world's first strategic jet bomber, the Boeing built six-engine B-47 was still experiencing growing pains in SAC, although declared operational. A lot of the performance data was still a slide-rule "guestimate" and the people who flew this mag-nificent aircraft had to improvise, often under extremely difficult conditions. To those who flew the B-47, you either loved it or hated it, but had to respect it or you didn't last very long. For those who didn't have the honor to fly the bird, a basic indoctri-nation is in order. The flight crew was composed of the aircraft commander (an impressive phrase, meaning the pilot in com-mand), the pilot and the radar/navigator. All three crew members sat in ejection seats; the AC (aircraft commander) and the pilot would eject upward and the RN (radar/navigator) downward. The pilots were in tandem, the pilot behind the AC. The radar compartment was in the nose, below and ahead of the AC.

The B-47 wings were flexible, designed to be able to move downward 14 feet and upward 12 feet, that kept the fuselage from buffeting during any turbulence. Number 2 and 3 and 4 and 5 engines were housed together in pods next to the fuselage and also the outrigger gear. Number 1 and 6 engines were outboard of the inboard pods. The main landing gear was in tandem, each gear having two large tires; the outrigger gear being housed below the inboard engine pods. This radical departure from the usual landing gear arrangement, that of two gear in the wings and a tail or nosewheel, caused special attention during take-off and especially on landing. If you landed with the forward gear touching first, the B-47 would "porpoise" or bounce back into the air, often to an almost uncontrollable condition. The key was to touchdown with the aft gear first, then gently lower the forward gear. Once in a porpoise, the only thing to do was pull the nose up, add maximum power and go around for another approach. In other words, you couldn't "spike" the bird on the ground. This was also due to the aerodynamically designed airfoils of the B-47, to actually fly on the ground, down to 60 knots. Landing at speed above 120 knots meant trouble and was always staring the pilot in the face, for the B-47 wouldn't "fall out from under you" as with most other high performance aircraft.

The B-47 was an unforgiving aircraft. A wrong decision anywhere during the flight, the results could be disastrous. You could end up with a bundle of trouble by a simple miscalculation. The "monster," as I reverently called her, traveled faster than anything I had flown before (primarily the B-17, B-25 and B-29) and the reaction time to decide what to do (and do it) was reduced to a split-second. Learning to fly the B-47 was better than with other planes, but the training couldn't teach the crew member how and when to react when the "big" decision had to be made. That came from experience, practice, practice and more of the same. Even then, every emergency couldn't be taught for the planning and training experts were still learning at a pace naturally slower than the people flying the "monster."

The B-47 is no longer with us, being overtaken by advanced technology, but it provided a test bed for the delivery of strategic weaponry today. It showed the world that jet aircraft could outperform and outdistance the then-present defensive systems. It also caused industry to respond to a requirement for more powerful fighter aircraft, capable of better performance and control.

I am proud to have flown more than 2,000 hours in the B-47 over a period of seven years. It was a beautiful airplane to fly, although very complicated. Its responsiveness was a pilot's delight. Once the gear and flaps (called "garbage") was up, the B-47 was a real performer and flew like a bird. It's too bad she has been retired to the bone-yard, but she made her mark in the world and I guess that's all anyone can ask of any piece of machinery.

One last thing about the performance of the bird. When the B-47 first was undergoing flight tests at the desert base of Edwards AFB, CA, the test engineers couldn't believe its predicted characteristics, so they setup a prop-driven B-29 and a B-47 with the same landing weight. Up to that time the B-29 was the most aerodynamically clean of any aircraft. The B-29 landed on the spacious salt flats of the southern California base and the pilots let it roll without use of brakes until it had completed its landing roll and stopped. Then they landed a B-47, letting her roll on her own. When the B-47 reached the spot where the B-29 had stopped, the B-47 was still going 115 mph hour! Man, that's streamlined. It also created special braking problems.

The memory of this beautifully engineered airplane will not dim in the minds of those of us who flew her. It deserves a special place in the history of flying machines.

* * * *

The first time I got close to the B-47, she was one of many sitting on the ramp at Pinecastle AFB, near Orlando, Florida. We were to receive the Training Command's flight indoctrination there. Officially, she was B-47B number 50-069, but to me she was the culmination of two years of training, waiting, missions over Korea, frustration and anticipation. Now on April 27, 1953 all the effort, the studying and interim tours of duty at Ellington AFB, Houston, Texas; Mather AB, Sacramento, California; Anderson AFB, Guam; Yokota AB, Japan and Travis AFB, Fairfield, California were now behind. This was to be the day.

All the pilots undergoing B-47 transition training at Pinecastle had undergone 14 months of intensive ground and air training, involving radar, navigation and bombing. Upon graduation were dubbed "four-headed monsters" (pilot, navigator, radar operator, bombardier) and having just completed 30 hours of flight training in the single engine jet training, the Lockheed T-33, for familiarization with jet aircraft operation. We had been taught all about the B-47 systems, fuel, hydraulics, electrical, propulsion, aerodynamics and on and on.

As Oliver (our instructor), Gene Peirson and I approached 069, the sweat was trickling down my back, soaking through my flight suit. We were carrying our crash helmets, flight bag and voluminous checklist. Because I didn't have the required total flying time (as a pilot), I was assigned as Gene's copilot by SAC. My primary job during this phase of training was mainly reading the checklist of the two pilots and familiarizing myself with the copilot's position by watching the instructor. I already knew I wasn't going to get much "stick" (actual control of the aircraft) time the first three flights, but at least I was in the bird and that was worth something, or so I convinced myself. We all had gone through the cockpit drill on the ground many times, but this was to be our first flight and even though I was going to be mostly a spectator, I was really going to be flying and looked forward to it with relish.

From my seat in the fourth man's position (below and to the left of the copilot, called "the hole," because you can't see outside at all). Motion and sound are the only sense you experience in "the hole." You just sit there with the checklist waiting and watching.

Gene was a good AC and we got along well. Once our Florida training was completed we were posted to Lake Charles AFB in the south central part of Louisiana. Once there we were assigned an observer, our crew training started and soon we rotated in and out of Goose Bay, Labrador for familiarization training. Soon thereafter, Gene was killed in a mid-air collision, flying with another crew at night and I was upgraded to aircraft commander, the first one in our wing to move from the back seat to the front.

Chapter 10

SURVIVAL/OVERSEAS DEPLOYMENT

Life as a flier in the military is not easy, or is it glamorous as often portrayed. As a matter of fact, it is a thankless, time-consuming grind, unless one loves to fly. Most crew members in SAC in the 1950s represented an investment of almost $100,000 (before inflation) to the taxpayers. As such, the military look to him to produce outstanding results. He is constantly under pressure and a multitude of other equally draining efforts are part of the everyday life. Huge responsibilities, endless training, much time away from home, endless paperwork and responsibilities incomprehensible to the average person. One of these is the survival training required of every combat crew, bomber or tanker. It is a requirement that cannot be dismissed. The Air Training Command holds the course at Stead AFB, Reno, Nevada and is fashioned after WWII prisoner of war experiences. There is a seven-day trek into the wilds of northern Nevada and California. With each crew is an instructor who is there to grade each crew member (we had 14 officers in our group, both bomber and tanker crews). We finished the seven-day excursion, but were given only three days of rations. What followed was an exercise that the crews were taken into east Nevada and told to find their way back to the base. The only problem was that we were escapees and the base personnel were the aggressors. If captured, the unfortunate ones were placed into a simulated stockade and had to do physical labor for 24 hours. It was not nice to contemplate.

Also, we were issued an accurate scale map of the entire area and a prismatic compass. Just before the convoy of trucks departed the base, we were given a special radio frequency and reporting schedule from which we would receive further instructions. It was assumed we would keep track of our location from the time we left Stead. This assumption was on the part of the instructors, for we were never told of this requirement and I'm sure it was done by design.

After a two-hour ride into the mountains north of Stead, the crews were dropped off at about five-mile intervals. There were about 20 crews involved in this particular exercise. They included B-47, B-36, B-29 and KC-97 flight crew members.

"Your first course is 315 degrees," the guide stated. "We go for 12 miles," he added and off we went. Our direction was generally northwest and we sighted in on a peak on our course. We settled down to a methodical 50 minute walk, 10 minute rest routine. We alternated carrying a 25 pound hand-operated generator every 25 minutes. At the end of my time period, that hunk of metal felt like it weighed a hundred, but it was our only link with Stead, so we bitched and cursed, but carried it.

Measuring distance by walking over any kind of terrain isn't too difficult. A nautical mile is 6,080 feet or about 2,030 yards; a normal pace is three feet, so when you walk 2,030 paces you've gone about one mile. Using the detailed map and with any luck, you can verify your position by landmarks.

"Okay, setup camp for the night. Be ready to start out at 0600 (6:00 a.m.) tomorrow." With that the guide walked off to find a spot of his own. He completely divorced himself from us during all phases of the trek. He was only there in case we got in trouble. He also graded each of us on our ability to survive and our ingenuity.

"Hey, Ray, what'd you get?" Our observer had been gone for over two hours, pompously saying he was going to get our dinner while we setup camp. He fancied himself as quite a fisherman, or so he told us. We had crossed a small stream sometime back and he was sure he had seen fish in the stream.

"They weren't biting today," he responded and then held up three good-sized trout, with a big smile on his face. Even the guide couldn't believe what he saw. Quite naturally, we didn't invite him for dinner. He had his own routine. Ray cleaned the fish, fried them and served them like any dutiful waiter should. They were delicious.

The next five days confirmed what I already knew, when you walk your feet get tired and when you don't eat you get hungry! Seriously, other than enjoying the out-of-door and the perfect weather and improvising when necessary, I felt the trek was wasted time. The real challenge was yet to come and I was eager to finish the survival march so we could get to the Escape and Evasion test. That thought helped pass the time quickly.

After returning to Stead, all the crews were given 24 hours to rest, eat, sleep and attend lectures on evasion techniques. We were being prepared for a 36-hour exercise, to test our capability to evade capture and return to friendly territory (the base). We were to wear our flight suits, boots, jacket, could carry no food and would be dropped off 18 miles from Stead out in the wilderness east of Reno. Our task: walk through heavily patrolled "aggressor" forces (Air Force Base personnel) conveniently stationed between us and the base. To show they were all heart, we would be given a one-hour head start before the "enemy" was turned loose to apprehend us (or so we were told, it turned out differently, as you will soon see). Oh, I forgot to mention we were to start at 11:00 p.m., but would not be told where we were starting from. If we were still "on the loose" when the sun came up, we would have to orient ourselves using a small scaled map! If it sounds like the deck was stacked against us, that was the idea.

* * * *

We left Stead by truck convoy promptly at 10:00 p.m., went through the main gate and turned towards Reno. On the northern outskirts the convoy turned left and followed a paved road for about 20 minutes, then left the main road, traveling on a rough road for another 30 minutes, then stopped. I kept these details in my mind so I could reconstruct our drop-off point. We were instructed to get out of the trucks and standby for our departure. Some 200 "escapees" lined up and were told to "go east when the first flare is fired." I quickly glanced upwards, found the North Star and noted we were already facing east. Just then a bright red flare illuminated the sky and we were told to "take off!" Imagine if you can, 200 men stampeding through the sagebrush at night. It sounded like a thundering herd, except for the cursing when one of the troops fell into a hole, or collided with another kindred soul.

About 15 minutes after the first flare, another flare was fired off to my left lighting up the whole sky. Those sneaky ___, I thought. We were had! Almost immediately I heard challenges being issued and it was shockingly apparent we were set up. The aggressor forces were waiting for us. I found out later, more than 125 of our group were caught in that initial ambush. I fell prone to the ground and rolled under a large bush etched against the bright light of the descending flare. I lay perfectly still for the best part of 30 minutes, hearing footsteps all around. Some were so close I could have reached out and tripped whoever was passing by. About 20 feet away a flashlight shone on an escapee. Another one caught, unfortunately. I was so mad at being suckered, I couldn't think of anything but beating them at their own game. The next few minutes passed quickly and the sound of moving men diminished, finally quiet surrounded me.

I moved cautiously from my hiding spot and almost immediately came upon a barbed wire fence, barring my way. My thoughts were still on what had happened and not on what I was going to do. It was almost a "fatal" mistake.

As I was crawling under the lower strand of the wire, a flashlight flashed on to my left and I was challenged by a gruff voice. I was so startled I bolted and took off as fast as I could. All of a sudden the ground was no longer there and I fell flat on my face in a dry creek bed! With the sound of running feet spurring me on, I rolled to my feet and moved back towards the noise following the contour of the dry wash. Shortly thereafter, I saw the "enemy" cross the depression, waving his flashlight in all

directions and then continued on. Fixed his wagon, I thought as
I was trying to catch my breath.

* * * *

Having walked up and down the hills until way after daylight, I stopped on the crest of a sagebrush-strewn rise, to rest,
collect my thoughts and try to figure where I was. I had sighted
several patrols in the last two hours, but it was all clear now.
Going back over the events, starting with our departure from
Stead, through north Reno, the dirt road, the time involved, our
initial heading of east, the dry creek bed, the valley and road
below me, all helped to formulate a general idea of where I was.
By closely checking my way, I was fairly certain I knew my position, about nine miles south of Stead. Nine miles to "freedom,"
I thought.

It would be very difficult to make my way through the lines
in daylight, so I decided to find a safe hiding place until dusk,
then it would be easier. Besides, the Nevada desert was hot. My
thoughts were interrupted by the sound of an automobile engine,
below and ahead. Just turning off the valley road was a jeep with
a driver by himself, driving up the opposite slope. My eyes followed the narrow road to the crest of a hill, where the road trailed
off into the sagebrush. When the jeep reached the top of the hill,
it stopped and the driver got out. I couldn't determine what he
was doing, but it looked like he was looking over the area. Then
it became clear to me, he was on high ground and had an excellent view of the area and approaches to Stead. Pretty smooth I
thought.

I noted the time, 9:30 a.m. The driver spent about 10 minutes
at his observation post, then got in the jeep and drove back down
the hill, finally moving out of my sight, around another rise in
the terrain. Just then I noticed three "aggressors" combing the
ridge to my left. Things were getting hot around here. Better get
away from this particular area. After carefully scanning the area
away from where I wanted to go, I figured I'd better get over
onto the opposite ridge for the sun was moving away from that

side of the hill causing shadows, which would be to my advantage. The area was clear so I made my way down the slope, using the bushes to cover my movements. Fortunately the ground was firm, so I didn't have to worry about falling rocks. I paused every few seconds, listening for sounds, then I heard a jeep engine again. Looking up the valley, I saw the jeep and driver again going up the ridge. Time was 10:30. He repeated the same actions he did an hour before. I wondered if a pattern was emerging. By God, if he was that stupid, then I'd be able to really "stick it to him" for the phoney-baloney they pulled on us!

When the jeep drove back down the slope and back out of sight the way it had come, I crawled down the hill, stopping short of the road, behind a rock. All clear, so I sprinted across the road, and dove for the cover of a large bush.'

Easing myself onto my side, I scanned the road, the ridge, above me and the far side of the hill I had just departed. There were the three enemy troops closing on the spot I had vacated minutes before. My luck was holding. I looked up the ridge and found the spot I was looking for, just below the crest where the jeep parked. Cautiously I made my way diagonally up the hill, keeping the three "aggressors" in view. They were busy combing the brush and weren't looking my way. I made it with no problem. Time was 11:15. Let's see if I had it figured right. A plan was formulating in my mind. I'd fix these clowns.

Carefully picking a spot where I could see the jeep and the road, I covered myself with loose brush, and relaxed, waiting for what I hoped would be a repeat of the past two hours. Promptly at 11:30 the jeep made its way up the road and parked on the crest. I was about 10 feet from the driver and could see his face clearly. A young AF lieutenant, all decked out in a crisp starched set of fatigues, his silver bar glinting in the sunlight. He scanned the area with his binoculars, but never down towards me. He was due for a big surprise if my plan worked right. Casually he lit a cigarette, watched his three troops across the valley for a minute, then slid into the jeep and drove off. I chuckled with what I had in mind for this one. It would take me about 30 minutes to set it up, and then we'd see. As the jeep disappeared from view, I scrambled up to the road, and moved parallel to it on the downhill side. I searched the upslope side of the road till I found the spot I wanted, about 50 yards down from the crest. Then I crawled to a point opposite a large rock pile and set up my plan. I took a large dry bush and placed it at the lip of the dirt road, piling a lot of rocks on top of it, then put several more dry bushes on top of the rocks. The troops across the valley had moved on and were no longer in sight, so I didn't have to worry about them any longer. To the base of the bottom bush I tied one end of a long length of parachute cord, which I had in my flight suit pocket. The time was 12 noon. I had to hurry. Laying down the length of cord across the road and up to the pile of rocks on the high side of the road. I then went back and covered the exposed cord with dirt, keeping my eye on the road. Finally, I took a piece of sage and brushed the loose dirt. Surveying my handiwork, I was satisfied and moved up behind the rocks to wait for my pigeon. Time was 12:15.

The plan was simple. After the jeep observer finished his trip and started on his way down the road, I was counting on the inexperience of the lieutenant to react to a particular situation, in my favor. He had to be the eager beaver type, but he had one glaring fault, he was predictable. At least this is what I was counting on. We would soon see,

12:30 and no jeep. If that kid didn't follow his routine, I'd chew dirt. 12:35, and there he was, chugging up the hill. I crouched lower and felt I could reach out and touch him. Was he due for a surprise! 12:45, here he came, slowly back down the hill. About 20 yards before he got opposite my position, I yanked on the cord, spilling the rocks downhill, making one hell of a racket, even over the noise of the jeep engine. The squealing of brakes gave me my answer. I looked up and saw the lieutenant jump out of the jeep, engine running, and ran down the slope, intent on capturing the "escapee." I reached the jeep in two strides, just as the bobbing head of the "pursuer" disappeared down the hill. Vaulting into the drivers seat, I shifted into low gear, and jammed down on the foot throttle. The jeep lurched ahead, fishtailing down the road, as I frantically tried to get it under control. Leaving a huge cloud of dust behind me, the car accelerated down the hill, leaving the eager beaver slipping and sliding to get his balance.

By the time I reached the bottom of the slope and turned onto the main road, I was doing about 50 mph. The jeep was slewing all over the road, and as I rounded the bend I could see the aggressor camp with several troops standing around, but no other vehicles. I was in luck, but didn't have time to relish the thought as I tromped down harder on the accelerator. I literally flew by those guys, showering them with dust and debris. I kept going until I was out of sight of the camp, then slowed down, pulling up on the top of a small rise. I could see the road from both directions. I caught my breath and my mind slowed down and started to review the situation. I had conned the "enemy" by distracting him, stole his jeep, ran through their roadblock, and now all I had to do was get on the base and reach the check-in point without being caught. I didn't know if the camp I overran was in radio contact with the base, but I doubted it. This road obviously led to the base, so I put the jeep in gear and started moving slowly along the road.

About two miles on the road I could see the orange and white water tower, characteristically the first thing that identifies a military installation. Next I saw some of the taller buildings and finally the runways, with an aircraft taking off. The perimeter fence was to my right, and the road ran parallel to it. About a half mile ahead I could see a gate and sentry box but no guard in sight. Then I remembered Stead was a Training Command base, and, unlike SAC bases, had no perimeter guard requirements. Man, I thought, I'm home-free.

After leisurely motoring to the check-in point, I parked the jeep about a block away and walked to the recovery building, signed in and immediately went to my barracks. No one else was there, so I flopped on my bunk and went to sleep almost immediately.

When I awoke some two hours later, there still was no one in the hut, but me. I found out later that most of those in our hut were captured within the first hour and the rest didn't even come close to getting back free. They all spent time in the simulated "POW camp," on the base. They carried railroad ties (each weighing about 60 pounds) from one end of the camp to the other, dug trenches, or were placed in boxes designed so the individual couldn't stand up or sit down. To add insult to injury, the guards would periodically pound on the box with baseball bats, much to the discomfort of those inside. Supposedly, the whole philosophy of the camp was to expose crew members to what they could expect if captured. Even with the guard towers, barbed wire, physical impositions, no food or water, and other inconveniences, it wasn't too realistic. You might say I didn't "play the game" by stealing the jeep, as the enraged commander said (there was supposed to be "none of that"), but then they cheated by starting the exercise before they were supposed to, so I figured anything was fair. I didn't even feel sorry for the lieutenant when he tried to explain how he "lost" a jeep.

Perhaps I had an advantage over the others, for, as a 20-year old B-17 bombardier in early World War II, I was shot down (November 1943). over German-occupied France, was captured, and escaped back to England, via Belgium, Denmark, and Sweden. But that's another story.

Chapter 11

DRAMATIC CHANGES

For the next two years we spent training, special weapons exercises, and, for me, two drastic crew changes. SAC's policy was a crew change only happened one per month. This was so crew integrity could be maintained and not compromised. That really was a joke. What it means is that, as an example, the radar operator is changed effective March 31, the copilot could be changed on April lst (March, then April, not the same month). A technicality, one that was not prevalent, but it happened to me. Our radar operator was going to school and had to be replaced. After looking at available personnel records, I decided on a AREFS young navigator, one lst lieutenant Harry Reitan, who had a good flight record with the tankers, and had a bachelor's degree from St. Olafs University in Minnesota. He was young and energetic. I made arrangements to have lunch with him at the Officers Club. When he came in, I liked him immediately. He wanted to get into jets, saying he was wasting his time in the tanker squadron. Quite forthright, and I liked that. He said he had trained on our radar set. I told him I would consider him for my radar operator. Two weeks later he was on my crew.

A similar problem surfaced with my copilot. He was selected for upgrading (I had recommended him, reluctantly) and I had to go through the selection process, all over again. Copilots are elusive people. Their background was critical on the B-47. They had to work closely with the radar/navigator and be ready to take over flying the bird if the occasion arose. He had to remain current in his pilot duties, and that wasn't always easy when his pilot wouldn't let him handle the controls. Unfortunately, it happened.

The man I tentatively picked was a Lieutenant Bob Tanner, who was a Texas ROTC graduate. He went to navigation school, then went to pilot school (his choice). He was assigned to our squadron as a spare copilot. He was perfect with what I had in mind. We talked for over an hour, and I hired him on the spot. I now had a crew, young, aggressive, and could handle themselves well in an emergency situation.

The crew changes brought a long delay in our being a top crew, but I was happy. There were other crews who were losing people, and it baffled me why my people were not snapped up even though I got into changes later. We had to go through an extensive number of crew and individual accomplishments to get to be combat ready, but I had gone through this twice, and knew the way to get it done. My first flight with "the new boys" was May 28, 1955, and we flew formation for the first two hours. I had Bob fly the aircraft for about 30 minutes, at which time he said his arms were tired. I took over control and told him to relax. Bob was like a lot of pilots with the B-47, he failed to use trim and to let things happen without manhandling the airplane. He had to learn, in as much as he didn't have much total flying time.

Harry practiced "station keeping" (flying formation on the radar scope, as well as where the other five aircraft were, in relation to the leader). Bob got so interested he asked if he could go forward and "watch" over Harry's shoulder. Good idea, I thought and told him to go ahead. For a pilot to express interest in what a radar/navigator does was significant. Even better is the fact Bob was a former navigator.

We were No. 5, so became the last aircraft to land. Our Wing policy was for every flight, the crew had to complete a jet penetration and either an ILS (Instrument landing system) or GCA (Ground Control Approach) to minimum altitude (200 feet) and a visual landing. We flew a GCA approach (weather was clear), and called the tower for a low approach that was approved by the controller.

"OK, Bomb, it's your aircraft. Complete the low approach and climb straight ahead to 2,000 feet. Harry, direct Bob to fly the downwind leg to base leg, and make a radar approach. Any questions?" The interphone was silent. I felt Bob take control, climbing to 2,000 feet, and reduced power so the airspeed held at 190 knots (structural limit with gear doors open was 195 knots, leaving the gear down. So far so good. Bob held the runway heading, but had trouble with the altitude. I told him to stop fighting the controls, and let the trim tabs take the pressure. About three miles out, Harry told Bob to make a slow turn to the left and roll out on the downwind heading (330 degrees). Bob complied, and he called for the checklist, I called the tower, and told them we were on an extended downwind (farther away from the runway), and asked them for other traffic.

"No other traffic, Blast 40. Call turning base leg. Altimeter 29.87, over." About three miles past the runway, Harry told Bob to make a 30 degree bank and roll out on runway heading. I waited for Bob to ask for the "before landing" checklist, again, and I read it out. He was a bit slow, but was OK. As we turned on the base leg (90 degrees to the runway), I asked if he was ready to complete the checklist. He agreed, and I told him the gross weight was 120,000 pounds, base leg 160 knots, flaps up.

"Roger, slowing to 160." He was still flying at 190 knots, much too fast.)

"Turn left to 150, on final approach," Harry directing the aircraft.

"Final approach to 130 knots, heading 150, full flaps." I was reading the checklist. He slowed to 130, dropped full flaps, and had a little trouble maintaining altitude. He said he was ready for landing. He told Harry he was taking over and going visual. He made a minor heading correction and dropped the nose, aiming for the end of the runway. The B-47 was tough to land from the back seat until you get used to it. As we approached the end of the runway, Bob had the aircraft under control, but his airspeed was 5 knots high.

"Bob, raise the nose, slightly. You don't want to touchdown nose first. You're in good shape." No response. He was concentrating and didn't want to take the time to respond. He wanted to land the bird. I thought later, this may well have been his first landing.

"Start your flare. Bring the throttles back. You're OK." Bob was holding his own and we touched down about 1500 feet down the runway.

"Chute," Bob yelled, and I pulled the parachute handle, and looked out of the rear view mirror, saw the chute blossom, and the aircraft noticeably slowed. I looked back at Bob, from the front seat mirror. He had taken off his oxygen mask and had a huge smile on his face. I gave him a "thumbs up," and told him I had the aircraft, as we moved towards the end of the runway. We turned off with no problem. As we taxied back to our parking area, I unlocked and cracked the canopy, letting fresh air blow into the cockpit. It felt really good. As we pulled into our parking spot, there was Staff Sergeant Vince Miller, a 22-year-old crew chief, and Sergeant Dick Baldwin, the assistant, behind him. I opened the canopy to the full open position and gave Miller a "thumbs up," telling him our plane was in good shape. He smiled and nodded his head.

When we were fully stopped and I had set the brakes, Baldwin opened the access door, and dropped the collapsible ladder. Harry was already handing down his gear, as I was getting out of the ejection seat and installing the safety pins. Bob was on his way out and I filled out the maintenance form and got out. Both Bob and Harry patted me on the back. They knew neither of them expected to do what I told them to do, without any warning. When we got back and out of the truck. In the briefing room I told both of them to sit down, that I had something to say.

"If you think I was pushing you, you are right. Bob, you did a fine job in landing for the first time. You were behind the aircraft for awhile, but caught up, and didn't panic." He looked at Harry and shrugged.

"If you want to follow me on the controls, especially during air refueling or landing, I have no objection. I'll try to let you land often. Not that I want you to leave, but you have to get the experience you need, and I have to believe you can do the job if something happens to me."

Not missing a beat, I turned to Harry and said, "you are the man, and I count on you to bring this crew to the top. I'll accept nothing else, and if I get the impression you are not progressing as I expect you will, you're out of here. Understood?"

"I'll give you 100% all of the time. Tell me what you expect from me, and I'll do my darndest to get it done. My goal is number one, and you can expect no less." With that, he relaxed and lit a cigarette.

"This will be a normal procedure for us, until we become combat ready. By that time, we all should know what to do before we're asked." I waited for a response, but they both nodded. I got up and went out. They did what they needed to do and that flight was history and a milestone. I set a standard for all of us and we were just starting.

Chapter 12

WHISKEY ORANGE, THE START

From March through April 1955, our crew melded, Tanner passed his standboard April 11, and Reitan passed his in May. We were Combat Ready. Our first mission after that was a Bomber Stream (one aircraft following another), meaning a B-47 every five minutes over a ground radar bombing site, then a night air refueling in formation, then an overwater (Gulf of Mexico) night celestial leg, and return to Lake Charles. It approximated an EWO (Emergency War Order) profile, that was something we all looked forward to. It was on April 22, 1956, called HOUND DOG, and we flew in squadron formation (Yellow Squadron), simulated bombing over Tampa, Florida, then refueled over Jacksonville, Florida, taking on 40,000 pounds, and finally our celestial leg, terminating over Brownsville, Texas.

We were scheduled to go to SES in May and passed the flights out of MacDill, with flying colors. We were upgraded to Lead Crew status, and that was personally gratifying. Bob and Harry walked around with a smile on their faces. We had a party at the Officers Club at MacDill and got very relaxed. The flight home was done in silence. Nobody met the aircraft and we went to our homes without incident. Strange how special occasions seem to go by the wayside.

We had passed the first hurdle, that of being recognized for our capabilities. I pushed the crew, and myself, to accomplish more than they had scheduled. If we were scheduled for two bomb runs, we would get three. If we were scheduled for a celestial leg, we tried to get two. On each flight we searched for a tanker, whether scheduled or not. Nine out of 10 times we completed a rendezvous and took on fuel to practice. We over-scheduled on each flight. As a result, we were designated Wing Crew of the Month in May, June and July 1956, for our achievements. In June we were selected as 2nd Air Force Crew of the Month, very inspiring, and made us feel we were heading in the right direction.

We kept up our activities into 1957, then I got promoted to major and Harry and Bob got promoted to captain. All three of us went on a 15 day leave (back in those days you took leave when you could get it). Bob, with his wife, Laverne, went to Austin and stayed with her folks. Harry took off for Minnesota, courted his sweetheart, Margaret, married her and returned. I was the only bachelor left and spent five days with my mother in San Francisco. I got lucky in wrangling a flight to Oakland, spent five days there and, through my mothers efforts, bought a Volkswagon "Bug," and drove it back to Lake Charles, alone. It took me three days, but I got back safely, exhausted, but happy. The only thing wrong with my new car was it wasn't long enough in the drivers seat. I am six foot three inches tall, but I really enjoyed the auto.

While we were gone, the Wing had to cycle in and out of the Lockheed plants in Marietta Georgia (Dobbins Air Force Base) to have each aircraft fitted with (the infamous) wing tanks by the Lockheed folks. That was a real shock, because of the inherent problems with the tanks. We flew several missions, ended up by landing at Dobbins, and returned with the installed empty wing tanks attached. Outwardly, the control of the B-47E was about the same, with the additional weight added another 200 feet of the takeoff roll and about two knots of increased speed on landing.

On October 6th, our crew led a flight of six on a daylight air refueling, called Shamrock Red, in the upper central United States. We hauled empty wing tanks. Harry did his usual outstanding job of guiding the formation to the tankers, in the area of Columbus, Missouri. We onloaded 12,000 pounds, then the six of us separated, and made simulated bombing runs on Omaha and Dallas. Our flight time was six hours and 40 minutes. We crammed a lot of requirements into a "short" flight.

On November 1, 1957, there was a Wing briefing. Harry, Bob and I rode in my VW. We thought it was another concerted effort to either have a bomber stream or a mass air refueling. As we approached the Wing briefing room we noticed the Air Policemen were very much in evidence, and that was not normal, but we would see, shortly, this was not something "ordinary."

Showing our flight line badges to the guard at the door, we found seats in the center of the briefing room. There was a large black drape lowered over what we knew to be a large pieced-together map of the United States. At precisely one o'clock, someone called "attention," and we all shuffled to our feet. The Wing Commander, Colonel Rohr, with the Director of Operations behind him, and the Wing Intelligence Officer behind him. That was strange. We rarely saw the DI at any briefing. Things were beginning to get tight. The thought came to mind that we were about to get into something very special.

"Gentlemen, be seated. This is a special briefing for all combat ready B-47 crews. It is classified Top Secret, and will not be discussed except in secure areas." The Wing CO paused, then started up, again.

"This will be the only Wing briefing for POP UP." A murmur went through the assemblage.

"Pop Up is the nickname for a new classified operational concept. Colonel Finan will continue the briefing. Raise the drapes, please." He sat down on a chair on the stage, and Colonel Bernard Finan stepped forward. I nudged Bob, and he tried to stifle a snicker,

"Pop Up is the nickname for SAC change from high altitude to low altitude strikes on enemy territory." He paused for effect. He was a former Public Relations Officer at the Pentagon and had a real flair for histrionics. He came from Washington, DC, to our Wing and was named commander of the 68th

Bomb Squadron. He did not follow orders, allowing himself as the final authority, which he was not. For some unknown reason, he was promoted to Wing Director of Operation, which made him all the more dangerous.

"The concept is for the B-47s to fly their EWO profile until we reach enemy territory, then descend to low altitude for the approach to the target.

"Each squadron will designate five Ready and Lead crews (not to include standardization crews) to fly the prescribed route and land back here." The DI was tracing the route with a pointer.

"Wing tanks will be removed, allowing us to fly at 425 knots. The routes and targets will be Oklahoma City, Dallas, and/or Little Rock. Pilots will not, repeat, NOT use the autopilot. If you lose an engine, abort the mission and return to Lake Charles.

"The squadron navigators will supply routes, targets to each crew selected to fly the initial missions. There will be no fourth man allowed. Any questions?"

A pilot from the 68th raised his hand and was acknowledged. He asked a question we all wanted to ask.

"Colonel, what is our flight altitude?" Finan had a haunted look. He looked at the Wing CO as if he needed help.

"500 feet above the terrain." injected Colonel Rohr. I never found out why the DO was hesitant to answer such a logical question. That was a dumb move in retrospect.

"The selected crews will takeoff at 0400 (4:00 a.m.) on the selected dates, because of the thermals you will encounter over Texas and Oklahoma in the late morning, at the low altitude. The first mission will be the 67th honor." Smile. Colonel Avery and the other squadron commanders did not participate in the flights. It was said they were needed to be able to assimilate and explain how the crews felt after the flight. The debriefing team will pay special attention to everything that we could communicate. After that little discussion, we were excused.

Lieutenant Colonel Lyndall J. Avery was our squadron commander.

He was tough, used a lot of profanity, but was fair above all else. He had flown with us several times, was an average pilot for one who did not fly much. He was fair and as long as you did your job, he left you alone. He was my squadron commander when I was selected to move from the back to front seat. I never forgot that.

The three of us came back to the squadron, and not a word was said by anyone the whole trip. I didn't know how Rob and Harry felt, but I was inwardly excited. Low flying was a thrill and I always felt a real pilot was one who could handle himself and his airplane at any altitude and speed. I hoped we were in the first five. When we got inside our operations building (on the flight line), for some reason we looked at the scheduling board, not thinking for one minute the "list" would be posted this soon. Surprise: There was the list of crews to fly the "pop-up" qualification missions. I knew they had to be instructor crews, so the "qualified" crews could teach the rest of the squadron. They were as follows:

1. Irvin. November 15
2. Waddell November 16
3. Snyder, November 17
4. Coleman, November 17
5. Goodman, November 18

My thought that the first ones would be instructor crews. Much to my surprise, my crew was the only one of the five who had instructor status.

I headed for Col. Avery's office. His administrative sergeant saw me coming, and using the intercommunication's phone, told the boss, "he's here." After a pause, he motioned me to the "old mans" office.

"What took you so long?" The boss returned my salute, puffed on his cigar, and leaned back in his swivel chair.

"Colonel, thank you for your confidence. I'm more than ready to lead the parade. I can hardly wait to put the bird through its paces at 500 feet, but what will the airspeed be?"

"Dave, I knew you were crazy, but I expected a little restraint. You go on the 15th. Your airspeed will be 425 knots. Any further questions?" There was nothing more to be said, so I saluted and left, heading for the squadron navigator's office.

He was putting down the phone when I came into his cubbyhole. "The Old Man told me you were coming. Reitan's already here and he's got the flight plan. What else do you need?" I turned and headed for the planning room. Both my people were looking at the flight plan, and didn't even look up when I trooped into their area with maps spread out on the table. I plopped down and said, "you can get downright embarrassing, doing what you just did." Harry looked up, smiled, and said, "Just trying to save you time. We knew you would be delayed, talking to Colonel Avery. You're so damned predictable." Bob never looked up, not wanting to get into the discussion. Doesn't sound like a Texan, but the three of us had accomplished a lot in a short space of time. They were both irreplaceable.

We were to takeoff at 4:00 a.m., November 16th, delayed one day because of weather conditions. The weather was forecasted to be clear and warm, that meant we would go. We could expect turbulence when we were abeam of Oklahoma City. It didn't sound critical, but we would have to see. Jets consume a lot of fuel at ground level. I needed to navigate the route. Our target, for the first flight, was the Oklahoma City railroad turn table. We were to climb to 18,000 feet from 500 feet, and fly at 425 knots. Harry computed our distance to start climb, level off, and gave himself 90 seconds to identify the target on the radar (the airborne bomber radar was extremely limited in range at low level, but got better around 20,000 feet, according to the Intelligence folks and bomb (simulated) when we reached the drop point. We would takeoff, climb to 10,000 feet and cruise over the Gulf until we were to depart our start point, Galveston, at 500 feet, and 425 knots indicated airspeed (474 miles per hour) or 6.4 miles per minute.

We were to fly under clear weather conditions, and report to the nearest FAA station every hour. The route was simple enough, but the biggest consideration was how well Harry's radar worked at such a low altitude. We had to stay clear of large cities or flocks of birds. The timing was not critical, because at 500 feet the wind was not a factor, so our airspeed was the only thing to be considered. In talking with the squadron navigator, he told us the reason we were picked to lead off the testing was that we kept good records, and the Old Man was very impressed with the fact that I had my own set of maps and kept a record of everything that went on. He knew our information gleaned from the low level flights would be invaluable to the planners. Not even the MacDill wings (they were the first to get the B-47) had flown any distances at low level, and no one had flown Pop-Up flights. So we would be considered the guinea pigs, but we were never told this information. The squadron navigator was a friend and he knew what we could do and didn't hesitate to tell us what was going on.

We discussed the altitude problem with the radar and Harry said the only problem was the range of the gear, plus being able to adjust the set during the climb to bombing altitude. He said he would have no problem with identifying the target when we were halfway through our climb. I told Harry I would follow his instructions and augment our location by pilotage (identifying our location by comparing the sightings with the low altitude flight charts). I told Bob he would be responsible for aircraft performance (engine, hydraulics, electrical, and airspeed), while helping me to fly at low altitude. The continuous pressure of aircraft attitude and high speed was really going to be a test of our stamina. I went to the training building on a daily basis and tried to build up my shoulder and arm muscles. As an after thought, I think it helped. On the 15th we had a briefing by the squadron navigator with the boss in attendance. Nothing new. The weather was to be good (I had already gone over the forecasted weather at the weather office at Base Operations), just a few low clouds above 10,000 feet at Oklahoma City. No problem.

Two of us were to fly the route the next day. I was to takeoff at 0400 and Snyder at 4:15, both to bomb Oklahoma City and return to Lake Charles. Our flight plan was nicknamed Whiskey Orange. The CO stressed the altitude and airspeed, and the need for accuracy in bombing, or the whole process was a waste of time. Like we didn't know that.

I didn't get much sleep, having to get up at 1:00 a.m. to make the station time at 2:00 a.m. When I got to the plane, Sgt. Miller was there, all smiles. He knew what was going on, having to remove the wing tanks, that, he said, was a real chore. Our being the first to go on a "pop-up." The maintenance crew was envious, and Vince promised he would talk to me and relay our experience information after the flight.

"Vince, how is the plane?"

"Ready, and glad to be without the tanks. They were a bitch to remove."

Bob and I completed the preflight, and Harry was satisfied with the radar operation. I told Sgt. Miller to cut off the GPU (ground power unit) and we would be back at 3:30 a.m. It was now 3:00 a.m. We took the long walk to Base Operations, made a last minute check of the weather, filed our flight plan and visited the men's room one last time.

After strapping in and getting the engines started, we called the tower and were cleared to runway 15 (southeast). "Call when ready," was their clearance, As we moved out of the parking area and onto the taxiway, I noticed Snyder and his crew standing by waving to us. I gave them a salute, and concentrated on getting ready for takeoff.

"Pre-takeoff checklist complete. Decision speed 115, takeoff speed 135."

"Roger, 115 and 135. We're ready to go." Got clearance for Pop-Up, Whiskey Orange, and taxied into position on the runway. Setting the brakes, I moved all six throttles to 100%. I turned on the wing lights and checked each of the six engines, visually. Bob said everything was "in the green," and I released the brakes. The B-47 started acceleration, slowly, as usual.

"Decision speed, NOW." We kept going. Everything was operating as they should.

"Takeoff speed, NOW." and I eased back on the yoke, and we were airborne, climbing to 10,000 feet. The gear and flaps were up, and we were ready for the big occasion. I switched the radio frequency to our control.

"Blast Control, this is Blast 32, airborne at 05. Whiskey Orange departure at 0500. Over."

"Roger, Blast 32, this is Yellow One (That was Colonel Avery's call sign). How does it look?" He sounded a little nervous. "Blast, we are under control. Take it easy."

Our first heading from Galveston at 350 degrees, and I maneuvered south over the Gulf, saw the lights of Galveston as contrasted with the shoreline.

"Radar's working okay. Galveston at 350, 30 miles." Harry, getting into the act.

Our speed was 425 knots, or six miles per minute and it would take us five minutes to get to the departure point. The time was 0552. I started a wide turn and started to descent on a heading of 350.

"Your timing is good, center the PDI (pilots directional indicator, that was transmitting the radar heading to my instrument on the pilots panel. It should be two degrees," I corrected and continued to come down to 500 feet. This was tricky because it was not yet light, and gauging height at night could be dangerous. Add to it being over water and it was doubly difficult. I watched my altimeter very closely.

"Over departure, at 0558, altitude 600 feet, airspeed 425, heading. Eta Lufkin 0607. Not too bad timing for a pilot." Harry adding his brand of humor. He knew he would get his due later on.

"How's the radar?" My question.

"Not too bad, range is about 10 miles. We're okay." Harry, the optimist, about halfway on this leg. It was beginning to get light and I saw Lufkin slightly to the left.

"Center the PDI," Harry had picked up Lufkin five degrees left. The indicator showed 10 miles. At 0607 Harry had us over the turning point.

"Turn left to 270. Waco at 0629.

I turned and settled in on 270 degrees, then said, "Bob take it for awhile. I want to check the fuel and consider what happened."

"Roger, I have control." He told me to relax. The first nine minutes from Lufkin went by so fast, everything was automatic. Thank goodness it was calm and clear. I tried to contact a radio station. "Any radio, this is Blast 32. Lufkin. Over." No answer. We were on time and fuel was transferring from the auxiliary tanks to the three main tanks and I gradually relaxed and stretched my arms.

We passed to the left of Houston County Lake, directly on course. I told Harry.

"Roger, we agree. Hold what you have."

When we got close, I saw Waco in the early morning haze. The sun was in our eyes, but the airfield runways were easy to spot. It was 0627.

"In one minute, turn right to heading 340. Wichita Falls at 56. We were one minute early. Not bad. This low altitude crap takes some getting used too."

"Shame on you," I chided him.

"Time to turn sport," Harry said. I told Bob to turn. He, concentrating, almost forgot. So Harry spoke and Bob started his turn to 340 degrees.

"Waco radio, Blast 32, Waco, at 27."

"Roger, Blast 32, Waco Flight Service Radio. Over."

"Waco, Blast 32, Waco at 27. Wichita Falls at 56, VFR, 500 feet." They acknowledged, and said nothing about the altitude. I wonder if they had been briefed on our operation.

As we passed between Mineral Wills and Fort Worth, I saw two commercial airliners going into the Fort Worth airport. Nothing else. I noted we were closer to Fort Worth than we should have been and advised Harry.

"Roger, hold at 340. I'll give you a correction as we get closer." I told Bob I had the aircraft, and he said his muscles were getting sore and was glad to turn it over to me. I could envision what would happen when we had rough weather.

As we rolled out heading northwest, I caught sight of a flight of F-86 jet fighters, above us and to the right. They were heading in the same direction we were. Bob saw them and said he thought they had seen us.

"Looks like they are trying to set us up for a tactical approach." Bob had taken some courses at Bergstrom AFB, outside of Austin, and remembered how the fighters were operated by the Air National Guard. They turned towards us and changed their formation to three flights of two aircraft, a standard situation, a leader and wing man, to protect the other aircraft. This was much the same as the Germans inaugurated during the Battle of Britain. They were still above us, but were losing their advantage of height. We were moving at a speed they had not encountered before. Bob said they were, in fact, Air National Guard F-86s.

The fighters made a tactical mistake of maneuvering to a point where they would be behind us. Making the mistake of misjudging our speed. They started down towards us, but lost the distance they wanted.

"Aircraft Commander, can I track them on our tail radar?"

"Pilot, A/C. Go ahead. Keep us advised. Harry make a note of our position and follow until they break off contact."

"Roger, I've already logged in what's going on. We are north of Mineral Wells, but I can't see Wichita Falls, yet." The fighters were from Dallas or Abilene. Their fuel could become critical if they tried to perform a tail chase. They did not have wing tanks.

"I have them at 7 o'clock (behind us and to the left), at extreme range (12 miles) and above. They're not getting any closer." Bob had turned around and was tracking the fighters on his radar set.

"Wichita Falls 12 minutes ahead," Harry with his estimate.

"Fighters behind and now losing distance. They'll never catch us at this altitude and speed." Bob said, with a happy note to his voice.

"Wichita Falls on the PDI, Center it. Turning point at 0651." It was now 0647. ETA Wichita Falls the same, according to Harry. He had the PDI showing three degrees left. I turned and stabilized the aircraft. We picked up a little turbulence, but we were under control.

"Wichita Falls radio, this is Blast 32, Wichita Falls. Over." We got in contact and gave them our ETA at Oklahoma City as 0723 (our actual "bombs away" time). As we passed over the Red River, Bob said the fighters had broken off and turned back south. They couldn't touch us. This made the low altitude penetration a reality, and protection. He had turned around and told Harry he was ready for the bombing checklist.

"Chickesea under the cross hairs, 30 seconds I disengaged the autopilot and started a fast climb. We were still at 425 knots. Our normal climb speed was 380 knots. As we passed 10,000 feet, Harry said he had Oklahoma City on the radar, and to center the PDI. He said to give him control. He really was ahead of the profile. I engaged the autopilot, except for the elevator, and then leveled off at 18,000 feet. Adjusted out attitude, and switched control to the radar operator.

We had passed to the left of Wichita Falls, turned right to 005 degrees (north), our ETA Chickasha was 0715, and Oklahoma City at 0725, so we were within "the window" the bomb plot was given. Our scheduled bomb release was 0724. Hopefully, Oklahoma City bomb plot was waiting for us. They had been briefed as to what to expect in the way of time and direction. I guess they were as nervous as we were. We had only 90 seconds till bomb release, so they had better be ready.

"Have the target area. It was 20 degrees to the right, so am turning, now." The aircraft turned to our new heading. I called bomb plot and gave them our crew number, target, altitude, and inbound heading. I had to retard the throttles, for the airspeed was too fast for our run. Harry said we should maintain 350 knots. The aircraft was stable, finally, and the altitude control handled the reduction in airspeed.

"Bombing checklist complete. Bombs away in 45 seconds."

"Oklahoma City bomb plot, this is Blast 32, over."

I was rushed, should have made that call a minute ago, but I was not ready, and probably couldn't have contacted them at a lower altitude.

"Roger, Blast 32. Ready to copy," He knew our heading and what target we were bombing, but I had to confirm it.

"Bomb plot, Blast 32, record run on target C Charlie, IP Chickasha, Heading 027, crew L83, true airspeed 425, bombs away in 45 seconds."

"Roger, 32. We are tracking you. Call 'bombs' away." Harry was listening and said we had 30 seconds. I was watching the "to go" timer and the bomb release light.

"Bombs away, Blast 32."

"Roger 32. Standby for your score." One minute Bomb plot called, and gave us our score in code. It was 300 feet at 10 o'clock. Before Harry could say anything, I said to him, "Let them shoot for that score, old troop." He agreed he would "take the score," and said it was because of his improved bombing technique. It appeared, as he and I discussed later, that the less time to identify and synchronize the target, the better it was, for him.

"We'll take it. Turning right to 160 degrees and climbing to 33,000 feet. I have an ETA of 0840. Does that sound OK?" He chuckled and said it was fair enough. He was tired and I couldn't blame him. He had a real workout and I didn't help too much, being late for my call to bomb plot. I checked the fuel with Bob and we agreed on 21,000 pounds. That would put us over home base with 13,000 pounds. As we got within 100 miles of Lake

Charles, I was tracking inbound on the local radio beacon and called Blast Control.

"Blast 32, Control. What is your location and fuel?"

"Control, 90 miles northwest at 33,000 feet, fuel 13,000 pounds (our lower limit was 10,000 pounds). We lowered the aft gear and outriggers to reduce the time to descend. At 2,000 feet, we were cleared for an ILS (Instrument Landing System) approach. The weather was clear, so no problem with the landing.

We turned off the runway, dropped the chute, cracked the canopy, and taxied back. Sgt. Miller was waiting along with Baldwin, and the truck to take us to our squadron.

I opened the canopy and gave Miller an "OK" sign, and he motioned us into our parking spot. Flight time: four hours and 20 minutes. Fuel: 9,500 pounds, cutting it close. No problems with the aircraft. It had handled the increased stress of high speed, altitude and turbulence well, thanks to the flexibility of the wings to absorb the bumps. Miller saw we were tired and carried our gear to the truck. I was thankful and said so. He saluted and went back to the plane to perform his postflight.

The debriefing took over an hour and was attended by Snyder, who was supposed to follow me, but his radar was not functioning properly and couldn't be fixed. He was scheduled for the next day if maintenance could get his set going. The Deputy Wing DO, the Wing Navigator, the Wing Intelligence Officer, and the Boss fired questions at all of us, but the primary recipient was Harry, and I wasn't worried about his being able to handle the queries. The Wing Navigator wanted to know about the shortness of the bomb run and the capability of the radar at low altitudes. Finally, Colonel Avery called a halt to the questioning. He told us we were scheduled in two days, and for the Wing people to read out post-flight paperwork, and that should answer a lot of their obvious questions. Our next schedule was for another route. This time we would bomb Little Rock. Obviously, the "big boys" didn't want us to get used to the "same" route, or they probably wanted us to check out various routes that would come down from SAC.

A RB-47E on the ramp at Topeka, Kansas. This was the reconnaissance version of the B-47. Note the electronic "pod" in place of the bomb bay.

Chapter 13

WHISKEY BLUE

The day after our first successful Pop-Up mission, we were briefed to go after an industrial complex in north Little Rock, to fly a circuitous route back to Lake Charles. Our flight plan was two 180 degree turns, that, at 500 feet, would be tough going, distance and timing-wise. After our bomb run we were to climb to 33,000 feet, and return, via New Orleans, to our base. This was Whiskey Blue

Initially, I was concerned about our fuel reserves, but we should get over the base with 10,000 pounds. It would be cutting us short, if anything went wrong. Our flight was to go over five hours, so I had to conserve my fuel where I could. Keep in mind, the B-47 Operators Manual provided optimum fuel consumption, based primarily on slide rule computations. Low level fuel flow as anticipated, but actual use had not been documented, so it was an estimate. We would add our actual use for future operations of this type.

On November 18, we again were scheduled to takeoff at 5:00 a.m. On the first Pop-Up flight I kept the airspeed high and only climbed to 10,000 feet. I talked with Bob, and both of us agreed that 20,000 feet and 250 knots would save us a lot of fuel, at the beginning.

Climbing to 20,000 feet, I made a short turn to the right (we again had fortunately taken off on runway 15 southeast), so we could be in the vicinity due south of Galveston, our departure point, again. It was still dark, but the lights of Houston were in evidence. Galveston was illuminated, and the coastline was a dark contrast to the city, as it was before. Having the same departure point was a definite advantage for us. Corpus Christi was indistinct to the west, or left of our orbit area.

"Radar checks OK and it looks good. First heading is 005."
Harry was satisfied and ready to go.

"Fuel transferring, electrical and hydraulics check OK. I saw
a plane off to our left." Bob, closing the loop. I turned on the
IFR lights (lights up the wings) to help identify us to others. I
started a slow descent (1,500 feet per minute) and kept us south
of the departure point. At 0555 (still dark) I positioned us 10
miles south.

"Center the PDI, timing looks good." The indicator showed
two degrees left, I decided to use the autopilot on this flight,
including altitude control. As we reached 500 feet I engaged
the autopilot and things went well.

"Our departure is on time, 0600. Not bad, for a pilot." Harry,
and his dry humor.

"Heading is 005 degrees. Shreveport at 0627."

"Houston radio, Blast 41, Galveston."

"Roger 41, go ahead."

Houston, Blast 41, over Galveston on the hour, VFR, 500
feet. Shreveport at 0629." They were clear but the level of their
transmissions were a little low. Couldn't expect any more from
this distance and our altitude. The autopilot was working fine,
allowing me to do some individual navigation.

As we passed abeam of Lufkin on our left side, it was light
and we had a little turbulence over the many lakes in the area.
The autopilot was doing great. The fuselage was very stable,
and the wings took up almost all of the shocks. I could see
Shreveport, still in the twilight ahead of us and slightly left.

"Center the PDI, I'm going to offset us on Shreveport, so
our turn will put us on course to Lufkin."

"Roger, three degrees right. Let me know when to turn."

"Turn left, heading 175 degrees, Lufkin at 36."

I turned the autopilot control knob and rolled into a 30 degree (a standard rate turn, as it is called) bank, noting I was
between Shreveport and Bossier City (home of Second Air Force
Headquarters and Barksdale AFB). I wondered if the tower op-

erators knew what was going on. I doubted it, but didn't worry about our "visit." I rolled out on heading, 425 knots, 500 feet.

"Shreveport Radio, Blast 41, Shreveport. Over."

We went through our routine reporting without incident. I did find out that the Barksdale tower personnel followed us on radar and called the radio station, and they were told we had reported in. The tower wanted to know what our altitude was, and were told it was 500 feet, under visual flight rules (VFR). There were no further inquiries. I hope the tower got used to it for they would have "visitors" every morning for quite some time.

Even with the offset, induced by Harry to stay within the authorized distance (10 miles), our turn put on to the right of course, and we were right of Lufkin, two minutes late. Harry had me turn right (instead of left) because of our position, and the fact we had another large turn. In my mind, Shreveport, Bossier City, and Barksdale AFB could be a problem for subsequent flights. He gave me a new heading, with an ETA of 0658. We had a few shocks from early thermal buildup. Probably would become a thunderstorm later in the day. The wings flapped, but we were steady in the "cockpit. The autopilot absorbed the abrupt movements with no problem.

As we passed Shreveport on the right and Longview on the left, we were about five miles off course. Harry came on and said to correct left to 000 degrees, Texarkana ETA would be 0659. We were three minutes late, and, if our flight plan included such time-consuming turns, we would have to compensate in the future.

I could see Texarkana ahead. We were on course. It was getting more bumpy as we passed over the foothills of the Ozark Mountains. We climbed 500 feet to compensate for the rising altitude of the terrain. As we were in the foothills around Little Rock, the turbulence abruptly got really rough. The autopilot was still handling the radical changes in aircraft attitude, but I had my hands full on the controls, just in case. I remember thinking the autopilot was handling the thermals much better than I could, and I would strongly recommend in my written report, and during debriefing, that the first Pop-Up flight fly the aircraft manually, but, after that, the pilot be allowed to use the autopilot, if he desired. Use of the autopilot would (1) maintain a more smooth aircraft control and (2) relieve the muscle problem that surely ensue and become a problem. As the low altitude and high airspeed mission progressed, I was ready to argue the point, that of safety of the crew, with the higher authority. This change would make the operational concept a real positive approach to our operational flights.

The wheels grind slowly at higher headquarters. My recommendation was not approved, but the operations concept "allowed" the aircraft commander to use the autopilot if he thought it would alleviate the stress. In other words, the AC could make his own decision, and, I suppose, that was a kind of approval. The pilots I talked to after qualifying for Pop-Up appreciated the use of the autopilot after the first mission. I believed (and still do) the first mission of this kind should demonstrate what the crew could be exposed to under less than optimum conditions.

"Over Texarkana at 03. Turn right to 030. It's getting rough down here."

"I'm climbing another 500 feet. It should stop a lot of the turbulence, hopefully." At our old altitude, the upslope reduced our stability, but, with the change of altitude, the buffeting became less. The planners didn't take into consideration the upslope winds that were prevalent at that time of year. It could only get worse during the summertime. This had to be taken into consideration, and I would make a point of stressing it at debriefing.

"Start your climb in one minute. Understand?" Harry was deviating from the flight plan, but I knew he had a good reason, and no discussion was appropriate at this time.

"Bob, get ready for the bombing checklist," was my response to Harry, and alerted Bob to what was going to happen.

At 0704, I started our climb to 18,000 feet. Harry and Bob were going through the checklist. It was my turn to get "busy." "Little Rock Bomb Plot, this is Blast 41, over."

Blast 41, Bomb Plot. We have you, climbing, inbound. Give us your bombing data, over." He was distinct, but a little faint.

"Bomb Plot, Blast 41, Heading 030, leveling off at 18,000. True airspeed 425 knots. Target M Mike, Crew Lima 83. Bombs away at 11. Will call at 30 seconds, over." They got the data. I noted Harry had picked up the target. The PDI showed left five degrees and 100 seconds to go to bomb release.

"I have the target area in sight. It's starting to breakup, Give me control, now." The bomb run was a bit erratic for Harry, but he settled down with about 40 seconds to go. Informed Bomb Plot of 30 seconds to go.

"Bombs away." The indicator light flashed. The time was 0711. We were a minute late, but nothing was said about that. "That should be a good one, I had trouble until the target was isolated." Our next heading was 160, with an ETA of 0811. Harry and Bob went through the "after release" checklist. It was OK, but Harry left the camera "on" so the ground people could verify our course and location. We normally would turn off the camera on our normal missions.

"Blast 41, Bomb Plot. Have your score. Are you ready to copy?" I acknowledged, and they said,, "Your score is Alpha Tango. Over." I smiled and unhooked my oxygen mask (the cabin pressure was 10,000 feet). Harry gave a score of 200 feet at 180 degrees. That should give the other crews something to shoot at. I told Harry and he didn't respond. I was climbing to 33,000 feet, and the thought of fuel consumption prayed on my mind. Our present fuel reading was 13,500 pounds. We should be over Lake Charles with a little less than 10,000 pounds. Cutting it close.

As I was leveling off and retrimming the airplane at 33,000 feet, Harry came back in the crawlway and his tousled hair told the story. He was tired. I patted him on the head, and he looked up smiling. I couldn't hear what he was saying because of the noise, but he was in need of using the relief tube. He went back and talked with Bob for a few minutes, then came back and patted my leg as he went into his "cubbyhole."

I homed in on New Orleans radio that showed us five degrees right. I corrected, and thought about the mission. We were over our turning point at 0811, turned right to a heading of 265 degrees, and estimated Lake Charles at 0840. After the radio call, I had Bob change to control frequency.

"Blast Control, this is Blast 41, over." They responded and took down my initial report. Then I dropped the "bomb" by asking to have the Wing Navigator meet us at our squadron when we landed. The controller said he would relay the information and request. I had Bob switch back to our approach frequency. We didn't need New Orleans Center's approval to descend, for under VFR conditions we had to be in the clear and were not under their control. The weather was clear and I vaguely saw the base, started down, and called the tower, asking for a GCA (Ground Control Approach) to runway 15. They switched me to approach control.

"Bob, you fly a GCA, I'll land it." I could feel his hands on the controls and he said he had "it." Approach vectored me to the altitude on an inbound heading. Bob asked for the landing checklist, and I read it to him. He didn't forget this time. He was a fast learner.

"Gear down, flaps down. Approach speed 120." We were down to 9,300 pounds, but I had the runway in sight. At 200 feet I took control and told Bob it was a good run. When the B-47 is down below 10,000 pounds on flare out, it has a tendency to "float" down the runway. The way to compensate was to flare at the approach end of the runways and the plane would normally land in the first 1,000 feet.

Chapter 14

WHISKEY RED

After we had been certified as Instructor Crews, as a result of completing five low level missions (three Whiskey Orange and two Whiskey Blue), we were cleared to fly with other crews (in the copilots seat, acting as an instructor; there were no radar operators or copilot instructor, a flaw in the system). It was a strange situation, because none of the Standardization crews were scheduled to check the squadron crews, and this was because the pilot and radar operators were supposed to be qualified in the Pop-Up maneuver, but none of the five crews who were to test the other crews in low level activities. Later, I discovered SAC considered the Pilot-AOBs were capable of evaluating the radar operators. This was a difficult position to be in. The only way to determine the capability of the observers was to (1) obtain the results of a Pop-Up simulated bomb run, and (2) have the qualified crew radar observer determine the technique of the evaluated observer. This included the low level navigation interpretation (to stay within 10 miles of course); to determine the radar focus, particularly during the climb from 500 feet to bombing altitude (he must change the position of the radar antenna on the aircraft, on a sustained basis), and, at the same time focus on the ground returns: extend the antenna to locate (search mode) the general target area. If, and when he identifies the specific target area (he does not select the specific target). That is done by the Wing Navigator on a rotating basis; in other words, the target was changed on each mission).

As the aircraft approaches the city and the general target area, the radar operator searches for the specific target area, and puts his radar cross-hairs where the target is specifically located. He is "flying" the aircraft heading, through the autopilot. The axis (heading) of attack can be different than the ground photos are concerned; that is the way of a target radar is displayed on the photographs (from previous runs by different crews) of the way the target area "breaks up" as the aircraft approaches the target area. At first the general target area, in a city, is a blob; as the aircraft closes on the target, it starts to separate and becomes more defined; the operator must react to changes, and be ready to put the cross-hairs directly on the target when it becomes the antici-pated specific point. The operator, who has looked at the radar film of previous/various targets in the Wing Navigator's briefing room. This phase of planning is essential for all radar operators, especially those who have less experience. They have a target folder they take on their flight, however the target photography looks completely different from that of a "normal" radar approach at 30-35,000 feet. At lower altitudes, target identification becomes more complicated and radar scores, generally, greater than can be expected, even from experienced crews, but have not been used to Pop-Up missions.

If a crew, under training conditions, without the copilot (in-structor evaluating from the radar seat) the change in bombing conditions can adversely affect the radar operator. I always felt sorry for the crew copilot, because he didn't get to fly the low level profile until the crew had flown three missions with the instructor and then only if they were declared as capable of fly-ing low altitude as a crew.

Usually, the training the crews underwent would mean they would fly Whiskey Orange or Blue. By far the most difficult, in the way of distance and targets were within the Dallas-Fort Worth complex. Departure was, as usual, Galveston. (I found out later this was a Federal Aviation Authority (FAA) input (more of a requirement), and that was because their identification of the low/ fast flying aircraft could be identified more easily because of an area radar approach radar just north of Galveston. The next check-point was 400 miles away at Little Rock. From there to Wichita

Falls was 420 miles, then to Mineral Wells (the initial point) 100 miles. It was the IP for Dallas target complex; Dallas to Lake Charles 250 miles. This was a total of 1,310 miles, all of it except 250 miles at low level. It was exhausting and cost the crew a maximum of coordination. This was Whiskey Red, and no crews wanted to be exposed to it. Dallas Bomb Plot targets were very difficult to identify. Target designator F for Foxtrot was an industrial complex northeast of the sprawling city of Dallas.

The best approach would be from the north, because of the target (in this case) being on the north side, thus reducing the ground clutter returns as the bomber is inbound. The worst direction of a bomb run on F Foxtrot would be from the west. SAC planners made it particularly tough by making the observers come in just north of Fort Worth, and over the main part of Dallas to get to the specific target. It looked as if the route and target "separated the men from the boys."

Most of the crews had trouble with Whiskey Red. New low level tactics are foreign enough, but to use the worst axis of attack put the crew at a terrific disadvantage. Several of the crews, new and old, needed extra training to get them through the Whiskey Red route. The reason for the elaboration is to demonstrate just how complicated a flight can become under difficult and pressure-induced planning and execution, to say nothing of going through the civilian/military airports on the way into the target area.

Whiskey Red route was introduced later in the mission requirements. Many believed this was done because the commanders got the impression the low level flights were "too easy," and had the Intelligence people use a difficult target complex and target system to further "test" the crews. This is my opinion, but it makes sense.

When flying with another crew as instructor, I had Harry observe the crews' flight planning and crew coordination. I relied on his intelligence and experience to assist me after the flight in determining the crews' capabilities, weak and strong points. I feel my responsibility as an evaluator was essential, and Harry agreed. He was a strong believer in strength and crew leadership.

One of the more important area physical considerations was elevation, that quite a few crews did not think of, primarily because all of the SAC flights were above 29,000 feet, where elevation was not a consideration. The low level route, except for Little Rock area, did not expose the new crews to elevations above 500 feet. West of Little Rock had a peak of 2,400 feet, and Whiskey Red route (from Little Rock to Wichita Falls) required the pilot to fly at 3,100 feet, then drop down to 500 feet. When out of the Quichita Mountains area, the pilot had to descend to a lower altitude. The key is always to remember the reason for the low altitude the reason being two-fold: (1) to stay under the enemy radar, and (2) prevent enemy fighter from making an attack.

The first low altitude mission of the crew I was flying with was a new combat ready crew. The pilot, a former copilot, but the navigator was new to SAC and the B-47. The copilot was a former tanker copilot, having little experience with jets of any kind. The whole crew was "under the gun," so to speak. They performed the preflight, and I met them at Base Operations, where they filed their flight plan. I had already checked the weather, and we could expect a medium deck (15-20,000 feet) of clouds from Little Rock westward to Wichita Falls, so we should not have a problem at our low altitude or during the climb to bombing altitude.

I briefed the three crew members that I would assist them when I felt it was necessary. Beyond acting as the copilot, my job was to evaluate their performance, considering the level of experience they demonstrated in the low level tactics and flying abilities.

We went out to the aircraft (53-2397) and settled ourselves in our ejection seats. I plugged into the interphone and waited for the pilot to ask for the checklist. We went through the startup procedure, and the pilot started the engines, and he called the tower for permission to taxi (I expected this; he was a former B-47 copilot and handled the radio instead of the copilot).

We would see how he acted in the air. The tower cleared us to Runway 33 (northwest), so we had to taxi all the way to the far end (Runway 33 or 150) we had to takeoff and then turn almost 180 degrees left to get into position over the Gulf.

"We'll level off at 10,000, and throttle back to 300 knots." The pilot spoke. I suggested they use 20,000 feet and 250 knots to save on fuel. He agreed, and asked the radar for a heading. I didn't understand what he proposed to do, especially when the radar was going to be very busy tuning the radar set, and being sure of our location. Now he had to keep track of where he was, where he wanted to be in order to come over Galveston on time and on the correct departure heading. I considered this to be poor crew coordination, and made a note to critique them.

The navigator made two changes in our position, in order to depart Galveston at 0600. Five minutes south the pilot announced he was descending to 500 feet, and let the airspeed increase until he got to 425 knots. At 500 feet (he didn't seem to have any trouble with his altitude; he must have been using the altimeter, and not watching outside the aircraft) he was slow to adjust the throttles to maintain his speed, and passed over the departure point two minutes late on a heading of 010 degrees (briefed at 015). The navigator did not announce the heading, or make a correction. We were heading directly towards Houston at 500 feet. The navigator, after we departed Galveston, told the pilot to turn to 015 with an ETA of 0659. The pilot turned, and called Houston Radio, reporting his position with an ETA at Little Rock.

It was finally getting light and navigation was relatively simple, but the pilot gave the navigator no assistance. We passed over the lakes between Lufkin and Shreveport, and were heading directly for Texarkana. That put us 10 miles left of course.

"Turn right to 020." The navigator. The pilot complied. His airspeed was 420 knots (five miles per hour slow, but not bad), We arrived over Little Rock three minutes late. "Turn left to 250." The navigator turned short of Little Rock (we had been briefed not to go directly over a large city at 425 knots and 500 feet. The civilian population would get quite nervous). Even turning short, we overran the course we were supposed to fly. We were on our way to Wichita Falls. I reminded the pilot he had to climb to 2900 feet to keep the 500 feet ground clearance. He pulled back on the yoke, and the aircraft climbed like a rocket. He overshot the correct altitude (2,900 feet), by 200 feet before he leveled off, and he lost 10 knots of airspeed. More importantly, the plane could have been within radar identification by an enemy.

The pilot got things under control and by the time he did, it was time to descent to 1,000 feet. The time to the next turning point was 0800, When we passed abeam of McAlester, Texas, we were five miles south of it. We should have been 13 miles south to be on course. Eight miles off course, but within FAA limits (10 miles). As we came abeam of Ardmore, Oklahoma we were still right on course. As we passed over the Red River (border of Texas and Oklahoma), and the next turning point, Wichita Falls, was 35 miles away. It was becoming visible to our left. Sheppard AFB was distinct, to the north of Wichita Falls. We were still right on course.

"Turn left to 165 degrees, ETA Mineral Wells at 0816." The navigator was three minutes late but didn't correct because of his being off course. I took control of the fuel panel and computed 9,000 pounds over the base. I figured 9,600 pounds, but that was close enough to have things under control. As an added afterthought, the Wing had a tanker orbiting north of our incoming heading, in case we had trouble with the gear or flaps. That was a standard procedure any time we were flying 'Pop-Ups." Couldn't complain about that, but it did give the crews a latitude that could help or hinder them.

The highway between Wichita Falls and Mineral Wells was a good signpost to follow. I looked down and saw the road to our left. We were still off course, but, if the navigator turned short, we would be in a good position for the bomb run.

At 0815 the navigator said, "In one minute turn left to 070 (Generally, East). Dallas at 0829. When you roll out, start your climb to 18,000." That young man had finally mentally "caught up" with the aircraft. The pilot executed a good turn, advanced the throttles and started to climb. I noted Mineral Wells to the right, as we passed 4,000 feet.

"Climbing to 18,000. Ready for bombing checklist." I was trying to help the navigator. As we approached our bombing altitude, the pilot engaged the autopilot, except for the altitude control. I read the checklist. The navigator responded.

"Leveling off at 18,000, airspeed is 425 knots." The pilot finally got into the act and called Dallas Bomb Plot, and gave them the information they needed.

"60 seconds. Pilot, GIVE ME CONTROL." The navigator with a rushed tone in his voice.

"30 seconds." The pilot called to bomb plot. They indicated the "had us," and call at bombs away. The navigator turned the aircraft 10 degrees right, but, from the back seat, I didn't know how much time was left. Usually, the aircraft should have been stable the last seconds.

"Bombs away." The pilot called out and bomb plot acknowledged, saying to standby for the score. The time was 0831. The navigator said to turn right to 135 degrees. ETA for Lake Charles would be 0916. It was time to relax.

"Blast 37, Dallas Bomb plot. Your score. Are you ready to copy?"

"Go ahead. Bomb Plot."

"Blast 37, Score is X-Ray Sierra Alpha." Our score was 3,400 feet at 12 o'clock (to the left of the target). The score was almost too far (3,500 feet was the limit), but, under the conditions they were under, the navigator/pilot team would accept it.

We leveled off at 33,000 feet and slowed to 250 knots. At 0850 we were 25 minutes from the base. The fuel was to be critical, if we had any trouble. During the entire flight, thus far, the pilot did not mention, nor did he ask what our fuel reserves were. As a former copilot, he should have remembered to keep abreast of how much fuel we had left, and, if he was going to be below the 10,000 pound limit, should have called for the tanker to standby in case of an emergency. The pilot tuned the radio compass to Lake Charles Radio, and the homing bearing indicator pointed 10 degrees left. He corrected and told the navigator. The radar was tuned to high altitude and the navigator said the base was under the cross hairs. No correction was necessary. Approach control told us to descend, we were only 50 miles from the base. A bit too close for us to be.

"Drop the aft gear and outriggers." said the pilot, I used the "emergency" gear lowering switch. The gear came down, but the left outrigger was still not down. I hastily looked at the fuel, 9,400 pounds. I told the pilot I had to leave my seat and "hand crank" the outrigger. The manual lowering handles were behind and to the left of the copilot, and he had to get out of his seat to operate the handle. The four handles (one for each gear) were about 14 inches long, that gave good leverage to manually extend the gear, I pulled the correct handle through its travel (about 25 inches) and started to pump the handle furiously. After about a minute the navigator hit me on the back (I had to face aft). I looked around and he gave me a "thumbs up." I had forgotten to reconnect the interphone cord and he had to come back from his position in the nose. I could discount my forgetfulness because of our fuel situation. I got back in my seat, saw the gear lever was down, and the indicators showed all gear "down and locked." I patted the navigator on his head and buckled myself in. So much for that emergency.

"On interphone." The pilot said OK, We were at 4,000 feet and 180 knots. Our fuel was 8,900 pounds.

"Am turning downwind for 33. Before landing checklist," I read it to him and by the time we were on the base leg, everything had returned to normal. I looked at the pilot's rear vision mirror and he had relaxed and was smiling at me.

We landed safely. I pulled the chute and the aircraft slowed; we turned off at the end of the runway and returned to the ramp. As we pulled into our spot, I read the fuel, for the last time, 8,000 pounds. Too close for comfort. Flight time five hours and 40 minutes. We finished the checklist and nothing more was said. The navigator got down, then the pilot, and finally I worked my way out. The crew chief came up to me, and asked what had happened. I motioned to the left outrigger and noted the down lock was now in place. Just in case, said the crew chief. I explained what happened, inflight. We looked at the gear housing. Nothing seemed to be out of order.

The flight crew was waiting in the truck. I climbed aboard and we went off the flight line, and dropped the crew at their operations. I told the pilot I could critique them at 10:00 a.m. the next day at his operations office. I told the driver to take me to the 67th Operations. The time was 10:00 a.m. A long day, but I still had to write what happened and, more importantly, if this crew should be allowed to fly a Pop-up without an instructor.

I talked to Harry and explained that the navigator wasn't "with" the aircraft until we got near the last low level turning point. I asked him to look at the film when it was processed, and to accompany me and critique the crew as far as the navigator was concerned. I told Harry I thought they should fly another supervised "Pop-Up," even considering that we flew the Whiskey Red profile. I reasoned that they needed to take some of the burden off the navigator. Harry agreed, without seeing the route and bombing film.

Chapter 15

OPERATION LONG RUN

The three bomb squadrons that comprise the 44th Bombardment Wing have been alerted for two days, and the briefing is about to begin. The Wing briefing room is jammed, all the seats are taken, and some of the latecomers have to stand in the back of the room. This USCM is different from others, in that both Lake Charles bomb units (44th and 68th Bomb Wings, 90 B-47s) and Air Refueling Squadrons (44 ARS and 68 ARS 40 KC-97s) will participate, theoretically exercising our capabilities as a cohesive package. This is not the usual routine, for each Bomb Wing (and supporting Air Refueling Squadron) has its own Operations Order, independent of the other unit on this base, but each form a part of the overall strategic posture.

As the briefing unfolded, the rain outside muffled the murmurs of the people inside. The huge map displayed behind the briefing officer (in this case the Division Director of Operations; DO, for short) tells the story: depart Lake Charles, fly to and land at Loring AFB, Maine, refuel the aircraft to full capacity, and prepare for takeoff the next day. Flying time: 3-1/2 hours. Takeoff from Loring: refueling over the St. Lawrence River, coast-out near Harmon AFB, Newfoundland, span the Atlantic, coast-in at Prestwick, Scotland, simulated bomb run at a specified target in France, and land at Royal Air Force Station Upper Heyford, England, flight time: 9 hours. Nothing was said about the return flight, which was extremely peculiar. Prior to this exercise, an overseas rotation briefing was accompanied by a return operation, but not this time. This USCM was taking on all the aspects of a highly interesting venture.

B-47E 51-5240. Back row from left: Harry Reitan, Radar Navigator; Robert Tanner, Pilot; author, Aircraft Commander. Front row from left: Assistant Crew Chief Norm Baldwin; Crew Chief Vince Miller (just before Texas League).

Once the Division briefing was completed, each of the Wing Commanders gave us a better-than-usual pep talk, but the crews were still not told anything about the return flight. We were all released for lunch and instructed to report to our Wing briefing rooms at 1400 (2:00 p.m.) for further specialized unit briefings. As we left the building, the rain had stopped, but the rainclouds persisted and were rather depressing to me. Harry, my outstanding radar-navigator, said he was going home for lunch. Bob, my copilot and well qualified to upgrade to aircraft commander, accompanied me to the Officers Mess. His wife worked, so he often ate on-base. While we drove the short distance to the Mess, Bob said, "I wonder what they've got planned for us after landing at Upper Heyford?" This was Bob's first overseas operation.

"I don't know, Bob, but it will be interesting to see what's going on. I hope we will find out at the Wing Briefing."

SPECIAL OPERATIONS

Because many officers were eating at the Mess, we had a problem finding a place to park, but finally moved in near my bachelors quarters, across the street from the Officers Club. We had to hurry, for the rain had begun again. The food line was very crowded, but Bob and I found seats with two of our squadron mates. Tex Jackson, an experienced B-47 AC in our squadron, asked me what I thought of the mission. My reply was that I thought we'd get more information at the Wing briefing. "I sure hope so," he replied. "It would be great if we could get a couple of days in London." Ray Hathaway, his navigator, smiled, knowing full well Tex had a "thing" about London. The last time we had spent time there together was in 1954 while on 90 days temporary duty in Morocco. Tex "did the town," and after a night of carousing, ended up climbing the flagpole outside the Columbia Club and the London police took a dim view of those antics, especially at 3:00 a.m. Fortunately, he got off with a reprimand, but he obviously wasn't deterred by the scolding.

By the time we finished lunch and got back to Wing Headquarters, the briefing room was already filling up. We found our crew table and our flight folders. Included in the sheaf of papers was the Operations Order, flight plan, communications sheet, air refueling procedure, and more. As we were going through the folder, the Wing DO rapped his wooden pointer on the podium, and the "Long Run" briefing was about to begin. Long Run was the nickname for the rotation to England.

"Gentlemen this is the final briefing for Operation Long Run," it began and what followed was a drawn-out, step-by-step analysis of the entire flight. The DO continued, "The 66th with lead off, with the first flight departing at 1030 local, tomorrow, followed by the 67th at 1100, and the 68th at 1130. Flight time will be about four hours and 15 minutes, landing at Loring. Prior to descent, be sure and advise the Command Post of the aircraft status." Each squadron was spaced 30 minutes apart so the landing base could handle the planes in an orderly fashion.

117

The schedule appeared to be real tight, and if the weather was bad, we could anticipate delays in landing. This wouldn't be critical, for the B-47E had an unrefueled range of eight and a half hours, under the best of conditions. The weatherman gave us an optimistic forecast. Only a 50-50 chance of snow, but the chance of fog was good, so we should plan for a radar approach, which we always did anyway.

"After landing, the "Follow-Me" jeep will park you, based on where maintenance wants you. Keep a close watch while taxiing at Loring. The snow drifts don't allow for much wing tip clearance. They've had 12 inches in the past 24 hours."

Bob leaned over and whispered, "I hope we don't have the same trouble we did the last time." I nodded and my memory went back to the previous February, when the squadron flew to Loring for a special weapons exercise. One plane landed too far down the runway, J.B. Reed couldn't stop and plowed into a snowbank, causing the other 14 of us to orbit in a snowstorm, under radar control. It took 45 minutes to get him off the runway, and when the last aircraft (we landed 5th) touched down the visibility was almost zero. We almost lost one that time.

"Crew buses will pick you up at the aircraft and transport you to your quarters. Aircraft commanders be sure to turn in all classified flight folders to the security officer before you bed down. We don't want to have a breach of security." This was amusing, because one aircraft commander left his classified crew flimsy in Base Operations when we left Morocco a year before. That caused quite a flap. Fortunately, the briefing officer happened to find the folder, called the Lake Charles Command Post and when the pilot landed, the Wing Commander blistered his backside pretty good. The responsibility of the Aircraft Commander in SAC, is all-encompassing. Not only does he have to fly the plane, he is also responsible for crew activity, coordination inflight and the ground training, but he is responsible for all classified papers, and that's considerable.

The DO continued, "Briefing for the overseas strike will be at the 42nd Bomb Wing briefing room at 0800, November 27. Buses will pick up the crews at the mess hall at 0745. All crew members will attend, including back-ups."

Each squadron sends a spare crew to the strike base, to standby as replacements in case a primary crew member gets sick or is incapacitated. Also, they help coordinate activities, such as messing, quarters, weather info, navigation data, etc. Their assistance in advance planning helps to make a more smooth operation. In this way their participation not only helps the planners but gives them a better understanding of what it takes to put a wing mission together.

The Wing Commander stepped to the podium, gazed at faces of the crews, cleared his throat, and started his pitch. "Gentlemen, this mission has been carefully planned, and all the supporting units are in place. For the first time we will be operating in conjunction with the 68th Bomb Wing. The timing of your landing is critical at Loring and Upper Heyford. The weather looks OK, but may take a turn for the worse this time of year, so play it careful. Don't take any chances. Safety is the first consideration, so keep it in mind. I'll be in the Command Post at Loring and Heyford until the last plane lands. If you have any trouble, call the CP. Don't wait until you've got a bundle of trouble before you ask for help. Good luck." Short and sweet, I thought, as we' were standing at attention while the staff trooped out.

Harry gathered up the paperwork for all of us and secured them in his briefcase. The three of us then headed for the squadron planning room to complete the flight plan. Harry and Bob went directly there while I headed for the flight line to check out the status of our B-47, No. 51-5240, nicknamed *the Prowler*. We had picked it up at the Boeing-Wichita factory brand new, and flew it regularly. Sergeant Vince Miller, the crew chief, was completing repair on one of the hydraulic pumps, while assistant crew chief Sergeant Norm Baldwin was completing the aircraft records, and standing near the ground power unit. Vince saw me coming and got down from the step ladder, wiping his hands clean of the hydraulic fluid.

"How's she look, Sergeant?"

"Major, I can hardly keep her from busting over the chocks, she's so ready," he smiled. No. 240 was like his own child. Although barely in his 20s, Miller had been working on B-47s for almost two years and was one of those rare mechanics who loved his job and was proud of what he was doing. He added, "We found a small leak around the seal of the left power pack, but its okay now. I've got my bags packed and ready to go. How's the weather at Loring?"

"They've got about five feet of snow, and the temperature's down in the teens, so be sure you've got you woollies with you," I advised. In SAC, the crew chiefs usually accompany their planes on an overseas rotation, unless they get replaced by a staff officer. This time he was scheduled to go with us and was looking forward to the trip. He was a pleasant companion and was helpful if anything went wrong. Vince also was an excellent coffee-server. You'd be amazed at the amount of coffee a B-47 crew consumes on a long haul. He didn't need to be told to have the two gallon jugs aboard they were always there, filled with steaming hot coffee.

"Looks like a good flight," I commented. "I don't have any idea how long we'll be in England, but maybe we'll get a couple of days in London." Crew chiefs get little enough compensation for their long and arduous work.

"I sure hope so. Word is the return trip will be a full scale operation," he said with a question in his tone. The flightline maintenance people never attend USCM briefings. They are only told where we're going and sometimes the amount of time we'll be on the ground, but they have their own methods of finding out what's going on. This time, however, he obviously knew no more than we did.

"OK, Vince, I'll see you tomorrow morning. You'd better get a good night's sleep. The trip overseas will be a long one."

March 1956: author receiving medal for outstanding service. From left: Colonel Talbot, 44BW Director of Operations; author; Colonel Robert Rohr, 44BW Commander.

At 9:30 a.m. on November 26, 1955, the weather was dreary and wet. It had rained off and on all night and this morning looked like more of the same. The base weatherman, usually optimistic in his forecasts, painted a gloomy picture for takeoff and landing. It looked like we were going to be on instruments most of the way, and Loring was down to 500 feet overcast and one mile visibility in snow showers, with no letup for our landing time. I hoped it wasn't a portent of what was to come. After filing my individual flight plan with the Base Ops dispatcher, I took another look at the Loring instrument letdown procedures, and that of our alternate, Plattsburgh, New York. Bob walked in with the flight lunches, and we had a few words about the weather, then walked out to the "Prowler."

"Laverne said to tell you she'll have some steaks for us when we get back," he said. I laughed, because that was a thing with us. Either Margaret, Harry's wife, or Laverne would pass on that invitation before a big mission. Many crews had similar superstitions, contrary to popular belief. Personally, I wouldn't fly without a medal around my neck that I got from my father. He got it in France in 1917, where he was an AEF flier, and gave it to me the day I graduated from flying school in 1942.

As we cleared through the flight line check point, we could see 240 in the second line of B-47s. Activity was going on everywhere. The blue maintenance trucks were everywhere, with the specialists doing their thing, trying to get one bird, or another, in commission. The mist reduced visibility, but the ground powered lights provided adequate illumination for the ground crews. Miller and Baldwin were finishing up their preflight and waved as we approached. Vince came down from the nose stand and said, "She's ready. No problems, 45 hours to go on the airframe before inspection." He was proud of that bird and the flight crews could tell. We trusted our ground crew. Unfortunately, not all ground crews were as conscientious as ours, They have their own checklists, but they sometimes missed an item, which could lead to big problems inflight.

The external power unit was providing AC and DC power to the aircraft systems and Harry was already in the nose compartment, preflighting the radar set, optical system, and navigation systems. Bob climbed into the crawlway, checklist in hand, and I followed. "Ejection seat pins in place and secure?" I twisted in the narrow crawlway, reached up and felt for the three pins, one for each arm rest, and one for the catapult charge, "three pins inplace and secure," I affirmed. Bob confirmed his pins in place, plugged into the interphone system and called for the inflight refueling (IFR) check. Vince answered on the ground interphone, "Standing by for refueling check," which meant he was on the nose stand, ready to check the lights and locking toggles in the refueling receptacle, located on the topside of the aircraft nose section. Harry said he was standing by to confirm hydraulic action of the pressure sleeves, controlling the toggles. Also, he could simulate the tanker boom seating itself in the receptacle by depressing the control valve.

The IFR check was completed without any problems. Harry said he was through with his checks, so I called for "power off" and Norm shut down the ground power unit. Bob and I started the external preflight check. Bob started at the tail, worked forward and completed his check at the right wing tip. I started my part of checking the aircraft at the nose, worked to the nose well, the bomb bay, and finally the left wing. I paid particular attention to the left power pack, but Vince did a good job with the former hydro leak, for it was clean and operated properly. When I was through, I went back to the tail and Bob and I connected the parachute lanyard to the retaining hook. The B-47 employed a parachute braking system to assist in slowing down the monster. This is one item the AC must do by order of the Wing Commander. If the chute fails to deploy on landing, the B-47 may not be able to stop using brakes alone. We closed the door, and locked the compartment, thus completing the outside preflight checklist.

The ground check took about 50 minutes, which meant we had some 30 minutes before we had to be ready to start engines, so the three of us walked the short distance to Base Ops for a final check on the weather, one final cup of coffee and to relieve ourselves if the urge required it. We updated the route weather cross-section and found Lorings latest weather teletype sequence was forecasting a slight improvement, which sounded good to us. Vince came in with the two coffee jugs, and I gave him a final briefing to be sure he was aware of what to expect. There were many things he could do, inflight, to help us out, and he knew we counted on him. Each flight crew used the "fourth man," as we called the passenger, for different functions. We were glad to have him along.

"OK, friends, its time to get ready, so let's move it," I said, and we all headed for the plane. Other 67th crews were scurrying around, getting last minute chores done. And there were the ever-present blue maintenance truck moving up and down the flightline, helping last-minute malfunctions to be remedied. Our squadron commander was talking to the DO in front of Base Ops. He had just checked with the Command Post, but there were no changes to the deployment.

The 66th planes were taxiing out on schedule. The noise was deafening as they went past us, then the noise died down as they moved down the long taxiway to the active runway, which today was southeast to northwest. This meant the takeoff would be towards us on the ramp. The rain and mist had stopped, so we should be able to see each B-47 as it lifted off and climbed into the low overcast. As we stood there, the lead planes' engines could be heard being advanced to maximum power, and it took about 10 seconds for the plane to reach a point where we could see it, accelerating down the runway. As it came into view, wing lights blinking, we could see the rain streaming off the wings. The first plane lifted off as the second plane's engines reached maximum power. As number one disappeared into the clouds, the second one came into view, and so on until the four lead flight aircraft had departed. Five minutes later the second flight took off. We were climbing aboard as the third flight became airborne. The rain started again. Its noise on the plexiglass canopy was faintly discernible as we put on our crash helmets, connected the interphone cords, and started down the checklist for engine start.

"Spiral Control, this is Spiral Olive Lead. Ready to start engines," came over the radio from the lead plane of our squadron. Number 2 and 3 called in, then Bob confirmed we were ready to go.

"Spiral Olive Flight, this is Spiral Control. Start engines."

"Bob, ready on No. 4?"

"Ready on 4. Voltage stabilized."

"Starting 4." I engaged the starter on No. 4 engine, the turbine wheel turned, the RPH gage indicated an increase, and, at 10% RPM, I brought No. 4 throttle into the idle detent, and the fuel and oil pressure rose, then the EGT (exhaust gas temperature) rapidly rose to 450 degrees centigrade, then lowered to a steady 300 degrees. Starting 5, 6, 3, 2 and 1, in that order, was a repetition of No. 4, and we were ready to taxi. The ground crew disconnected the external power. The Prowler was now on aircraft power.

"Spiral Olive flight, this is Olive leader. Go to ground control frequency for taxi instructions. "This was followed by verbal affirmation of each of the flights. Bob switched channels.

"Ground control, this is Spiral Olive Leader, with a flight of four. Request taxi instructions. Over."

"Roger, Olive leader, you are cleared to taxi to runway 33. Altimeter setting 29.80. Call when ready to take the runway. We have your clearance when ready to copy. Over."

"Roger Control. Olive flight, taxi in takeoff order." As Bob acknowledged, I noted the No. 1 aircraft slowly started forward, following the "follow me" jeep through the other parked aircraft and was followed by No. 2 and 3. When No. 3 passed us I signaled Baldwin to remove the wheel chocks, added power to all six engines, released the brake lock, and swing into line. When taxiing behind another jet aircraft, you have to maintain a respectable distance to keep gravel and debris from being thrown into your engines by the plane in front of you. A pebble can nick a jet engine rotor blade, causing the engine to become unbalanced and could do extensive damage to the inner workings, necessitating the engine to be shut down.

The checklist items continued. Harry indicated his set was "on" and in good condition. Bob rechecked the takeoff information and relayed the latest data to me. Takeoff distance was 8,500 feet.

"Olive Leader, we have your clearance. Call when ready to copy." Apparently the ground controller thought the leader had forgotten. Not likely.

"Roger, control. Go ahead. Olive flight, copy."

"Spiral Olive Leader and flight is cleared to the Loring airport. After takeoff climb to and maintain flight level 330 (33,000 feet). Turn right after takeoff, climb on course, Contact departure control after turning on course." The No. 1 aircraft repeated our clearance, and was cleared to tower frequency. We all switched channels.

"Lake Charles tower, this Spiral Olive leader with a flight of four. Clearance received. Request permission for takeoff. Over,"

"Roger, Olive leader. Temperature 50 degrees, wind 310 degrees at 12 knots. You are cleared for takeoff. Have a good flight. Over."

"Spiral Olive flight, this is Olive Leader. Maintain one minute separation for takeoff. Leader taking the runway." The number one taxied onto the runway, lined up and advanced power to 100%. He rechecked his instruments and released the brakes.

"Harry, check our time. I'll tell you when No. 3 starts his roll," I told my boy. "Don't I always?" was his instant reply. That was his way of relieving the pressure. With everything going on around you, light flashing, the rain on the canopy, the noise, the anticipation, the checking and rechecking of the instruments, you can get pretty wound up.

No. 2 started his roll, then No. 3. As he started, I advised Harry and moved into position. Harry started counting down in 10 second increments. At 30 seconds to go I advanced the throttles evenly to full power, watched the instruments, stabilize. All within limits.

"5, 4, 3, 2, 1, start your takeoff, now!"

"Roger, rolling." I released the brakes and we started moving. The B-47, weighing 180,000 pounds of which 80,000 pounds was fuel, accelerates very slowly. About 2,000 feet down the runway, we're going only 95 knots. At 8,000 feet it reaches a takeoff speed of 145 knots. Unlike a lot of aircraft, you can't "pull" the B-47 off the ground. With tandem gear, it won't fly until its ready, so you just ride it out. At 120 knots the flight controls begin to take effect, and at 145 knots she flies herself into the air.

"Gear up," I called at 150 knots.

"Gear coming up. Standing by for flaps," Bob responded.

"Flaps up," at 160 knots.

"Flaps coming up. Gear up."

The bird was accelerating rapidly. A B-47 pilot must be very careful, immediately after takeoff. If he gets distracted or is not concentrating on the airspeed and forgets to get the front main gear up by 195 knots, the gear doors will peel back like an orange. Once you get the "garbage" (gear and flaps) cleaned up, the B-47 is in its element. She's so sleek that you have to be careful, or she'll accelerate beyond safe airframe limits. When the airspeed reaches 310 knots, you gently raise the nose and maintain that speed. We were in the clouds and on instruments through 8,000 feet, climbing at 5,000 feet per minute, and suddenly we broke out of the weather, into the almost-blinding sunlight. This never ceases to send a shock through your system. It's like coming out of a long dark tunnel into the sudden daylight. I lowered my tinted visor to reduce the effect of the sun.

"Time to turn on course. Heading 075," Harry called out. I started a 30 degree bank to the right and rolled out on the desired heading and started looking for the three planes ahead. Bob was looking over my shoulder but the distortion of the canopy and the blinding sunlight kept him from seeing them. We had a station check, passing through 10,000 feet. Everything was OK.

"Harry, better start station keeping. I can't see them, yet."

"Roger, I have them at 12 o'clock, four miles and above." The radar can pick up aircraft, if properly tuned, and the operator knows what he's doing. The rest of the flight was straight ahead of us. Harry spoils us, for he knows what's expected of him, anticipates what is needed, and really works at his job. He's a gem.

"Olive flight, go to interplane frequency and check in," directed the leader. Bob switched to a special frequency, called the leader and asked for his position. This got us away from the standard chatter on the common radio frequency.

Each aircraft checked in, then the leader indicated," 15 miles southwest of Greenwood VOR at flight level 310; 3 and 4, do you have me in sight? Over."

"Three, Roger. I'm three miles back. What is your airspeed?"

"Roger, three. Leveling off at flight level 330, airspeed 245."

"This is Olive Four, five miles back at flight level 280. Have you on radar, but no visual."

"Roger 3 and 4, will throttle back to 230 until you catch up."

"Dave, I've got all three on the scope. No. 1 and 2 are to-gether, No. 3 is two miles back, and we're four miles, directly behind, and closing OK," Harry announced. At this point I raised my visor and immediately saw the planes ahead, and told Harry to relax. "Vince, how about a cup of coffee?" "Coming up, boss," was his immediate reply. As we leveled off at 31,000 feet, I let the airspeed build up, engaged the autopilot, checked the cabin pressure, unhooked my oxygen mask and took the coffee from the crew chief's hand.

"Let's have a station check," I said, the crew chief checked his position, followed by the radar operator, then the copilot, and then me. Additionally, Bob and I cross-checked our instruments for accuracy. I started fuel transfer and slowly reduced speed as we moved into position to the right and behind No. 3. Standard loose formation in SAC is the leader on the left, and the others to his right and behind him, in designated sequence,

"Olive flight, this is Lead. Over Greenwood at 06, turning to a heading of 084, increasing speed to 245 indicated." Greenwood, Mississippi, radio beacon (VOR) was our first turning point. Next would be Nashville, then Charleston, West Virginia, Scranton, Concord, and, finally, Bangor, Maine. Bangor VOR would be our last checkpoint before letdown into Loring. We would get the latest weather from Bangor Radio. At that point the decision would be made to go on (if Loring weather was okay or divert to our alternate, if Loring weather was below landing minimums. This time of year, in this part of the country, you never know.

The flight was uneventful up to descent. The weather was good at our altitude, except we never saw the ground because of a blanket of clouds below us. We checked out the short and long range radio equipment for accuracy, used the equipment and cross-checked its accuracy with radar fixes. The time was well-spent, for we were going to be over the Atlantic for six hours on the flight from Loring to England, and wanted to be sure all our equipment was operating. If not, we would get it fixed at Loring.

Chapter 16

LETDOWN AND LANDING

"AC, this is radar. Letdown point in 10 minutes," Harry advised. Bob and I went through the descent checklist and waited for Olive Lead to call for descent. I turned down the temperature in the cabin, to keep the canopy from frosting over or fogging-up when we descended into the denser, warmer air near the ground. This was a trick I learned to do from past experience. Now it was just a matter of time.

"Olive flight, this is Lead. Go to approach control frequency and standby for instructions." We all confirmed and Bob again switched channels. The radio frequencies had been preset by Bob on the ground at Lake Charles.

"Olive flight, this is Loring Approach Control. We have you in radar contact. Olive lead, descend and maintain 20,000; Olive two, descend to 21,000; Olive three, descend to 22,000; Olive four, descend to 23,000. Each aircraft acknowledge and report reaching assigned altitude." Each of us reduced power, and descended from 33,000 feet to our designated altitude, slowed to 200 knots and reported in. We were now vertically spaced for our approach. To expedite our approach, Control then cleared us en route to 4,000, 5,000, 6,000, and 7,000 feet, to report over the Loring VOR.

After the other three aircraft were cleared to GCA (Ground Control Approach - radar landing system) frequency, it was our turn. "Olive 4, you're cleared to descend to 4,000, turn right to heading 180. This is your downwind leg," instructed approach control. Radar was spacing us on a heading parallel and the reciprocal to the landing runway (36, for 360 degrees).

"AC, this is radar. You are 10 miles east of the runway, parallel" confirmed Harry. He always followed through with his radar and could guide me down in an emergency.

"Thanks, Harry. Bob, let's start the Before Landing Check but we'll hold the gear till we're established on the base leg."

"Olive 4, turn right to heading 270. Complete before landing check. This is your base leg. Contact final approach control on channel 17."

I turned right to the assigned heading, which placed us 90 degrees to the runway heading, completed our checklist and contacted the final controller. "AC, this is pilot. Gross weight 110,000, approach speed 120, base leg speed 130" Bob advised, after taking a final fuel reading. I slowed the aircraft, lowered the gear and stabilized the aircraft to fly at 130 knots.

"AC, this is Radar. Expect time to turn to final in 15 seconds," Harry advised. There he was, again.

"Olive 4, this is your final controller. Turn right to heading 355; weather at Loring is 800 feet overcast, one mile and snow flurries; wind 340 at 15, altimeter setting 29.84, temperature 19. We have you on centerline, 10 miles from runway, check gear down and locked. Glide path in three miles." The weather surrounded us, but we could intermittently see the ground, although snow was pelting the aircraft, and we were picking up ice on the wings and engine nose cones. From now on the conversation would be one-sided, ground radar would orally vector us and we would physically respond without saying anything. I was beginning to sweat, and my left hand, on the control column, was gripping the wheel with unneeded strength. I relaxed.

"Olive 4, start descent, turn left to 345. You are 20 feet low, on centerline." The controllers voice was electric, and shook me. I raised the nose slightly, and added power to maintain approach speed.

"Olive 4, you are 10 feet low, turn right to 347 degrees, two miles from runway." Good correction, I thought. I leaned over and turned on the landing lights with my right hand and switched on the windshield wiper. The snow was obscuring the windscreen. The aircraft was trimmed properly, responding to my touch.

"Olive 4, on glide path and centerline. Excellent correction. One mile from touchdown. You should see the strobe (high intensity) lights. If you have them in sight, advise." A pause for my comment. I saw the lights, but not the ground, so made no reply. I lowered the nose slightly, and reduced power to maintain the approach speed. My palms were sweating, and I consciously loosened my grip on the control column. Almost got it made, I thought.

"Olive 4, one half mile from touchdown, minimum altitude is 2000 feet. If you don't have the runway in sight at that altitude, pull up on present heading climb to and maintain 4000, contact approach control on channel 15. You are now one quarter mile from touchdown, 100 feet from minimum altitude."

I saw the strobes, then the green boundary lights, then the runway thresh-hold lights, and maneuvered for landing. At the same time I punched the interphone button. "Bob, I have the runway, standby the chute," I called. Upon touchdown, I brought the throttles back to idle, Bob deployed the landing chute, to help decelerate the aircraft. When the chute blossomed the effect was abrupt (like stomping on the brakes of your car). Our restraining harness kept us from bending too far forward. When we had slowed to 100 knots, I gently applied brakes to test the runway conditions. No skidding occurred, so I applied increasing pressure, as Bob called off the available runway remaining, as marked by large numbers at the side of the runway.

"3000 feet, 90 knots." I could see the end of the runway ahead, and I braked harder. It was a futile effort and I knew it. The Prowler was under maximum braking action now, but it made me think we were slowing faster than we were. Snow flakes swirled and splattered against the windscreen.

"2000 feet, 70 knots." Still moving too fast to allow me to turn off the runway at the cross-taxiway, but we almost had it made. Bob was sweating it out, too, for he had depressed the intercom button without realizing it, and I could hear his fast breathing.

"1000 feet, 50 knots." My God, we're going to make it. I immediately moved the steering control from "takeoff and land" to "taxi," and gently steered the bird towards the left side of the runway and the final taxiway. I almost laughed aloud. Here we were in below freezing weather and the sweat was running down from my forehead.

"Damn, this turkey didn't want to slow down," Bob blurted. "I sure thought we were about to end up in a snowbank."

"Or worse," added Harry. At that moment I appreciated Harry's eternal problem of not being able to see what was happening on the ground.

He could only feel the bird moving and felt helpless, sitting down there in the "hole." He often said the feeling was almost enough to make him want to be a pilot, but not quite enough he hastened to add. His personal philosophy, I often felt, was that you had to be crazy to be a radar operator, but to be a pilot you had to have more than a few "loose nuts" between your ears.

We turned off at the end with everything under control. Bob changed channels to ground control. We stopped, dropped the chute, and received instructions to proceed to the parking area. Normally, I open the canopy to get some fresh air into the cockpit (inflight the cabin is pressurized and air conditioned, but it's not the same as direct fresh air), but this time I kept it closed, to keep out the snow, moisture, and cold. It was, after all, 15 degrees above zero on my outside temperature gauge, and that's cold.

"AC, this is radar. Radar and nav equipment in commission. I don't want them to touch it." advised Harry.

"Olive 4, this is ground control. After parking, contact the command post." Bob changed channels.

"Afford Control, this is Olive 4, over."

"Roger, Olive 4, confirm aircraft and systems in commission." We acknowledged, switched off the radio and shut down all aircraft systems.

As our engines wound down, Vince opened the pressure door, released the collapsible ladder, and started handing down our gear to the ground crewman who had already opened the outer door. As was our custom, I departed the aircraft first, with my flight bag in tow. The Wing CO stepped forward and shook my hand, saying transportation was waiting and we would get further instructions at our quarters. The bus was empty, having already deposited the other crews at the transient quarters earlier. We climbed aboard after telling the crew chief to refuel and tie down the Prowler. Flight time was four hours and 20 minutes. I signed off the maintenance log, which told maintenance the aircraft status.

The short ride to the BOQ revealed nothing but snowdrifts and dim outlines of buildings. By this time the snow was really coming down. I wondered if the 68th Squadron would be able to get in, they being inbound 30 minutes behind us. Better them than me.

As we pulled up to the entrance, the driver indicated the mess hall was across the street, within easy walking distance. That was helpful. The three of us ran for the entrance and almost collided with the Wing Navigator, who was trying to hold the door open for us. He showed us our bunks and indicated there would be a meeting tonight of all aircraft commanders at 2000 hours (8:00 p.m.), and a briefing and flight planning session tomorrow morning at 8:00 a.m. at the Base Operations planning room. As it was now 6:30 p.m., he suggested we have dinner, pick up our gear, and the bus would pick me up at 7:45 at the BOQ. We deposited our gear on our bunks, washed up and walked across the street to the mess hall, still in our flight gear and parkas. The snow had stopped but the wind had picked up. It was biting cold, and the wind went right through our clothing like a knife. shivering as we entered, the smells of food warmed us, and we noticed most of our other crews were already there in various stages of eating their dinner. I noticed the squadron CO was not there, nor were any of the wing staff. This was rather peculiar, for they usually were stuffing their faces before the rest of us. After we had filled our food trays, cafeteria-style, we found an empty table, next to Tex and his crew. The warmth of the mess began to help me to relax.

"Dave, what's going with a special briefing for us?" another AC asked me, as I passed his table.

"Beats me. Sounds like something special is going on. Where's Si (our CO)?"

"He was picked up by Rip (Wing CO), Colonel Rohr, when we landed, and I haven't seen him since. Maybe he's over in the VIP quarters." Each base has a set of quarters reserved for high ranking officers, sort of away from the "riffraff."

Harry, Bob and I ate in silence, each with our own thoughts. Harry finally broke the silence. "After we landed, the Wing Nav was particularly inquisitive about our radar status. He's never bothered with that before."

Bob mused, "Something's going on. Did you notice the 44 ARS KC-97 parked in front of Base Ops?" Each air refueling squadron has distinctive markings, and we already knew our tanker outfit was in place at Goose Bay, Labrador, in anticipation of our deployment to England.

"No, I didn't notice. I wonder who's on board to be able to park in front of Base Ops." The flight line ramp in front of the base operations building is normally reserved for ranking officers. Bob shook his head and Harry was more interested in his lemon pie than our conversation.

After our second cup of coffee the time had come for me to go to the special briefing, so I left my people. The other ACs were already waiting in the bus, and when I climbed in, the bus driver closed the door and headed for base ops. I sat next to Jack, my flight commander, a longtime SAC pilot, and older than most of us. Usually quiet and imperturbable, he smiled at me and said, "Dave, I've been in SAC since 1948, and I've never seen anything like this. A simple USCM doesn't go like this one. I'm afraid we've got a special mission going." There was nothing I could say to that, so I shook my shoulders and kept quiet.

It was still snowing as we pulled up in front of Ops. I saw the Division Commanders aide talking to our Wing DM (Director of Maintenance) just inside the doors. Now, for sure, something was up. I nudged Jack and nodded towards the pair. "Oh God," he exclaimed, "for sure something's going on." The fact that our Division CO didn't like B-47s was a standing joke. He never flew one. He contented himself with an occasional flight in the prop-driven KC-97. His appearance here indicated something special. We were soon to find out.

* * * *

As the last of us entered the briefing room, the Air Police guard forcefully closed the door, from the outside. I had the fleeting feeling of being trapped, like being in jail with the rest of the pilots. I wondered if it was an omen of things to come. As I found a seat next to a 68th pilot, I could see the Division and Wing Commander in the front row, with the staff next to them.

Everyone seemed to be talking at once. The noise level was like a slap in the face. The looks on most of the aircraft commanders reflected the apprehension I felt.

"Gentlemen, PLEASE take your seats, and QUIET DOWN," the DO yelled in his loudest voice. It took an unusually long time to quiet down the pilots and the DO frowned. "You have been asked here independently because of the nature of our forthcoming USCM." The noise level rose appreciably, and the DO frowned even more deeply. "Up to now nothing has been said about our return flight to the states because of security." He had a flair for the obtuse, and we all knew it. Come on, quit stalling, I muttered. The AC next to me heard it and nodded.

"Upon arrival at Upper Heyford, all crews will stand down for five days." This brought an immediate positive verbal response from the crowd. I immediately looked for Tex. He was all smiles. "London here I come," he whispered, his grin spreading from ear to ear. The general feeling was much the same.

"Allright, you animals, quiet down. What I am about to tell you will not be discussed except with your crew. Above all, do not talk about it near any strangers, or any military people except those you know." He stopped, and let it sink in. We all fidgeted in our seats. Let's get on with it, I mentally urged.

"On December 5th, elements of the 44th, 68th, 301st and 376th Bomb Wings (180 aircraft) will execute an unannounced strike on selected targets in the US from bases in the United Kingdom. No flight plans will be filed and Air Defense Commands will not be informed of the strike force. The primary function of this mission is to test the capability of SAC to penetrate Continental United States radar defenses and of our defense forces to protect our country from a massive strike. The nickname for this exercise is Texas League." Pause, for effect, no doubt. "Simultaneous strikes will be mounted from Morocco and Alaska. SAC's plan, as directed by the Joint Chiefs of Staff (JCS), is to saturate our borders with bombers. This coordinated attack has never been done before on such a large scale. You must impress on your crew members that any leak in security will cause a loss of impact on this mission. Offenders will be subject to a court martial. Security Services will be involved, but have been told nothing of the strike. If you are caught by them you can expect to pay the consequences."

The United States Security Service (USSS) with headquarters at Kelly AFB, San Antonio, Texas, is the watchdog of military activities in the U.S. They have specially-trained people everywhere. They continually monitor inflight radio communications, attempt simulated sabotage on SAC bases, and try to obtain factual data on our operations.

They correlate all information available and present their findings to the CINCSAC (Commander in Chief, Strategic Air Command), which shows how good our security is. They are constantly playing games with us and we are constantly on the alert for them. On one occasion at Lake Charles, a checkpoint security guard on the flight line was suspicious of an officer wanting to go on the flight line. He had a flight line pass, but his identification card picture didn't match his face, so the guard told him to disrobe, spread-eagle on the ramp and not to move. The guards' carbine must have looked like a cannon to the officer, for he lay like a fallen statue. After calling the Security Command Post,

the guard firmly planted his GI shoe in the small of the un-
clothed individual and waited. It was 2:00 a.m. and 20 degrees,
but the man never moved. As it turned out, the officer was an
impostor, a penetrator from Security Service. He was duly carted
off to the Security Police office, vehemently protesting his handling. He was one of a team trained in the job of penetrating
SAC's defenses, and with the ultimate goal of "sabotaging" our
planes. His task was to first gain access to the flightline, then
put a slip of paper (marked Bomb) in as many B-47s as he could.
Fortunately, the alert guard foiled his chances. Score one for
our people. Part of the units' capability and effectiveness is
measured by the ability to provide protection against sabotage.
The units never know when a penetration operation is going to
be leveled against it.

"The flights will depart Upper Heyford at 30 minute intervals, exit the UK at Prestwick, refuel over the Greenland Icecap,
then head southwest to the breakup point. Each aircraft will
then depart on its own individual flight path, striking targets in
Detroit, Chicago, Milwaukee and Cleveland and return to Lake
Charles. Refueling onload will be 45,000 pound (6.5 pounds of
jet fuel equal one gallon of regular gasoline), flight time 11
hours and 30 minutes. Flight profiles will be provided each crew
at Upper Heyford. Final crew briefings will be 0900 (9:00 a.m.)
on December 5. Save your questions for the crew briefing."

The DO stepped down and the Wing CO, still in his flying
suit, stepped up, took the pointer, and traced the route on the
large map on the wall behind him.

"You will notice that our USCM route has several jogs to it.
This is to keep us out of the Canadian Early Warning Radar
sectors until we have been established on our individual tracks
about one hour. We don't want to alert the Air Defense fighters
until the last moment, then it will be too late for them to catch
us. Stick to your flight plans, and don't cut any corners. The
weather at Goose and Harmon is marginal, so we may have a
delay on departure. It's too early to get a good forecast now, but

will have a tanker scout in the refueling area 24 hours before the strike. Plan your flight carefully and don't take any chances. I'll see you in England." Our boss stepped down. The General stood up, and, in company with the staff, walked down the aisle to the main exit almost before we knew what happened.

We all boarded the bus and no discussion took place. The driver was a civilian, so each one of us knew we couldn't discuss the developments of the last hour in front of him. He could conceivably be a Security Service man.

* * * *

"Well," Harry greeted, "are you going to tell us what's going on or do we have to start guessing?" I motioned them to sit down on my bunk. We got our heads together and I told them the story, from beginning to end.

"Looks like a hairy one," Bob said. "I guess we can expect radio silence from takeoff to the target area. That ought to stir up a hornets nest."

"I hope the tankers can handle the cycling. If there's weather, we all got a big problem, "Harry commented. He obviously was thinking of our last USCM, when we refueled over Nova Scotia, and everyone had a hell of a time getting their fuel. Last February we had to rendezvous between cloud layers, and the turbulence was wild. We never did get our scheduled amount of fuel. One highly experienced AC threw up in his oxygen mask, it was so rough behind the tanker.

The B-47 has an unlimited range with its capability of refueling inflight. The receptacle is recessed on the right side in the nose. In 1955 the only refueling aircraft for the B-47 was the KC-97, a 4-engine prop-driven aircraft. This was several years before the KC-135, four jet engine tanker, the military version of the Boeing 707, was operational. The transfer was accomplished by a 20 foot telescoping boom slung under the aft body of the tanker. The boom operator "flies" the boom into the B-47 receptacle, by means of stabilizing fins on the boom. Transfer of fuel, under pressure provided by four pumps, was approximately 4,000 pounds (or about 615 gallons) per minute. Once the boom was seated in the receptacle, pressure from the tanker pumps opened the B-47 refueling valve, and fuel poured into the tanks of the B-47. The refueling "envelope" (maneuvering space behind the tanker) was five feet left and right of the tanker centerline, five feet up and seven feet down. The telescoping boom allowed for fore and aft play of five feet. It sounds easier than it is. It's a hard, demanding job, and the AC finishes a 20 minute contact sweating all over, and his muscles are bowstring tight. The slightest instability causes the B-47 to whip around like its on the end of a swinging rope. It takes the utmost coordination on the part of both the receiver (B-47) and tanker (KC-97) to complete a successful sustained transfer. Try, if you can, to imagine moving 180,000 pounds two feet, and you have some idea of what confronts the B-47 pilot. It takes about 20 minutes of continuous contact to transfer 40,000 pounds of fuel. As the B-47 takes on more fuel, the tanker must reduce the pressure because there is less area (in the B-47 tanks) to fill with fuel. It takes more time to get the last 10,000 pounds (about one hour of fuel at cruising altitude) than the previous 30,000 pounds.

The refueling altitude was from 14,000 to 21,000 feet, dictated by the tankers, altitude/power/weight limitations. The B-47 gulps fuel at an alarming rate at low altitude, consequently the less time at low altitude means more effective use of its fuel reserves. As an example, we burned about 10,000 pounds per hour (for six engines) at 35,000 feet, versus 20,000 pounds per hour at 20,000 feet.

Chapter 17

DEPARTURE FOR THE UK

After a good night's sleep, breakfast was especially good, and I was hopeful it was a good omen for the mission tonight. The weather outside had cleared and it looked as though we weren't going to have any trouble during refueling.

"Bus will leave in five minutes," the bus driver announced, to no one in particular. The bus, as usual, was crowded, what with all the gear for each crew. It got stuffy with all the people crammed into such a confined space, but fortunately the trip was a short one. As we entered Base Ops, one could see the flight line crammed with B-47s, and the ground crews were all over the planes. There was no question that the mission was "go," for all the activity. Ground power units were snorting their black smoke, while the maintenance people were checking the aircraft systems.

As we took our places in the briefing room, the DO was on the platform ready to begin. Once everyone had settled down, and without any frills, he began. "Orange flight will depart at 1755 (5:55 p.m.), rendezvous at 1855, refuel and proceed on course at 1925; Blue flight will follow at 1825, rendezvous at 1925, on course at 1945; Olive flight, takeoff at 1955 (7:55 p.m.), rendezvous at 2055, depart on course at 2115. Scheduled onload for all flights is 40,000 pounds. Flight time will be eight hours and 40 minutes. Controlled landing times at Upper Heyford are included in your flimsy. Each crew will start a night celestial navigation leg, departing the coast and terminate at Prestwick. Weather?" The weatherman stepped forward.

"Weather on takeoff should be 2,000 feet broken and five miles visibility; refueling area clear and unlimited; no significant weather en route. All the weather will be north of your flight path. Weather over France is low overcast, solid; weather on landing might get rough; Upper Heyford is forecasting 500 feet and one mile in fog and haze. Alternates to the north, indicated in your flimsy, should remain good for two hours after scheduled landing times. Your weather flimsy includes winds aloft, weather profile along the route, and alternate weather for landing time. Radar Navigation?"

The Wing Navigator stepped up. "Each crew flimsy includes target assignments for each aircraft, photographs and other data. Flights will breakup over Prestwick and proceed individually to IPs (initial points), bomb runs start from a known point, usually not more than five minutes from the target. Your respective routes will space you for proper landing times. Operations?"

"Expect flighter intercepts from Air Force and RCAF (Royal Canadian Air Force) aircraft until coast-out. Pine Tree radar will monitor your progress until you're 100 miles past coast out. If you have any problems Pine Tree should be called on GCI (Ground Control Intercept, radar) frequency. The locations and frequencies are in your communications flimsy. Any questions? No, OK. You're free to get on with your flight planning. I'll be standing by at Base Ops if you need anything. I'll be in the second aircraft and see you all in England. That's all."

* * * *

Flight planning for our crew is a very serious business. Harry had most of the work to do inflight; Bob, a former navigator, knew what Harry wanted and they worked out the route together. I was also a navigator before becoming a pilot, so I was aware of all the planning required. The more alternatives we planned for, the easier our flight would be. While Harry and Bob laid out the route and filled out their flight plans, I made up my own. The only difference was I plotted the radar sites, airfields with runways long enough to handle a B-47, and position reporting locations.

"We'll plan for a coast-out time, 10 minutes after the scheduled time, to allow for a late refueling," Harry announced." Our first fix will be 15 minutes after coast out." I can get a good radar fix as we leave the coast then have time to adjust for the initial celestial fix."

"Sounds like a good idea, Harry. I'll get a three-station fix from the Canadian radio stations in the area," I offered. "We can also get a fix from Ocean Station Bravo and Charlie, if we can raise them." Navy picket ships were permanently located near our route, and they could provide us a fix (with their onboard radar) if we could establish radio contact. Their positions were identified in the Radio Facility Chart handbook, available to all pilots.

Two hours later we were satisfied we had done our homework, and were the last ones left in the briefing room. The AC's don't usually make up their own flight profile, and most of the navigators don't precompute their star fixes.

"Bob, what do you have as a landing fuel," I asked. "25,000 pounds," he answered. "If we subtract 10% for a buffer, that'll give us 22,500. If we plan on the farthest alternate (Prestwick), that'11 give us 12,500 there. Based on a minimum of 6,000 pounds at Prestwick, we could take on 34,000 pounds and be in good shape. Sound OK?"

"You bet. We'll make that the minimum onload on the fuel curve. The more we can get the better off we'll be."

"Right, but we'll have to break off at the end of air refueling orbit or the tankers will break it off. We'll play it as it comes, but I'll try for a fast hook-up, so we can start refueling fast." That settled we went to lunch, then turned in for a few hours nap. We had a long night ahead of us.

* * * *

Harry and I loaded our gear aboard the Prowler while Bob was at the flight kitchen, getting our flight lunches. I told Vince we would delay the air refueling check until the copilot returned. I ran a complete outside check but a hurried one. It was cold and the wind was chilling me to the bone. Already the first flight was taxiing out, so I climbed in the nearby maintenance van to escape the weather and have a hot cup of coffee. When Bob arrived, we completed the checklist and climbed into the bird, strapping into the ejection seats, pulling the safety pins and waited until it was time to fire up.

* * * *

"Ready on No. 4, "Bob called, as we waited for the leaders, call. The engine start and taxi out went without incident. As No. 3 started his roll, we moved into position, lining up on the centerline of the runway, and set the brakes. I advanced the power to 100% on all six engines, methodically cross-checking all instruments. The Prowler was vibrating as if to say, "let's move."

"Ten seconds." Harry called out.

"Everything normal," Bob said, verifying my readings. I released the brakes and we started to accelerate, moving smoothly down the darkened runway, noticing the pile-up of snow on the grass of the runway.

"Decision in 10 knots," Bob called out. Suddenly the No. 5 engine fire warning light came on. The shock at seeing the red light startled me, and I chopped the power to idle on all six engines, automatically, without thinking, hit the brakes hard, and called out, "Fire warning No. 5. Check the engine, Bob." I couldn't afford to divert my attention from stopping the 90-ton monster to see if we actually had a fire or not. The light went out when I reduced power. I deliberately didn't deploy the chute, in case the fault was not an actual engine fire, and we could still make it on another takeoff attempt. It took about 15 minutes to reload a new chute.

As I slowed and turned off at an intermediate cross-taxiway, Bob confirmed no fire. I called the tower for a maintenance truck and permission to taxi back to the takeoff runway.

"Roger, Olive 4, the maintenance truck is waiting for you. What's the problem?" As I was taxiing down the parallel taxiway, I explained the malfunction, knowing the maintenance people were listening on their truck radio. Vince, without being told, had already opened the inner pressure door, and, as we pulled up in the run-up position, the maintenance people were running towards the plane.

I unhooked my oxygen mask as the line chief entered the crawlway. I yelled to him to check the engine for signs of a fire. His assistant heard what I said and was down the ladder and checking the outside of the engine with a flashlight as I checked the engine instruments. Nothing wrong there.

I got an "OK" signal from the ground crew, then I signaled I was going to run a full power check on No. 5. As I advanced the power, the fire warning light flickered, but didn't stay "on." At 100%, everything appeared normal. I moved No. 5 throttle back to idle.

"Chief, pull the panel and check the electrical sensing leads," I instructed the line chief. He was already on his way down the ladder with Vince right behind him.

In the early days, the B-47's engine electrical circuitry sometimes caused faulty readings. The pilots were familiar with these erroneous readings, and our crew chiefs knew exactly where to look. I turned on the IFR (Inflight Refueling) lights to illuminate the wings and engines, and saw Vince giving me the "thumbs-up" signal, indicating everything was under control, then signaled me to check the engine at full power, again. At 100% rpm, the No. 5 engine gave normal readings on the instruments and the fire warning light stayed extinguished. I signaled a "thumbs up" so Vince and the line chief re-fastened the engine access panel and moved out of the way, Vince literally ran up the ladder, closing the inner door and quickly connected his communications gear.

"The warning electrical connection was loose. It's reconnected now. No signs of fire. Ladder is stowed, outside door closed and locked. I checked all No. 5 five engine access panels secured." Short, clipped statements told me all I wanted to know.

"Roger, Vince. Good show. We'll try it again."

"Tower, this is Olive Four. Malfunction corrected. Request permission to take the runway." The tower acknowledged, the maintenance truck moved out of the way, and we again lined up for takeoff.

"We're down about 2,000 pounds and seven minutes behind," offered Bob, as we went through the before takeoff-check.

"Roger, understand" I answered. "Harry, I'll turn directly on course to the refueling point. Maybe we can shave a couple of minutes that way." He acknowledged and gave me a new heading to fly. I advanced power on all six, everything was normal, and released the brakes. This time everything was OK and we were on our way.

The takeoff and turn on course was normal. I kept the power at higher-than-normal settings, hoping to get into formation as soon as possible. The night was black as the proverbial ace of spades, and we saw almost no lights on the snow-covered ground. I stayed on instruments. We were over the sparsely populated area of southeastern Canada. The weather was crystal clear and cold outside, but inside the Prowler the temperature was a comfortable 70 degrees. We were at least 40 miles behind the others, by my mental calculations.

After what seemed an eternity, we reached our assigned altitude and I trimmed the aircraft, engaged the autopilot and suddenly was very tired. I didn't start fuel transfer because to empty the auxiliary and wing tanks would take longer to refill than the main tanks. Because of our pre-planning I knew we had a comfortable reserve of fuel. Right now I was more worried about getting back on schedule than the extra fuel we were burning. I felt sure we could take on the extra fuel needed and still arrive at Upper Heyford with a safe reserve.

I tried to relax and take stock of the situation. The Prowler was in good shape, and I concentrated in conserving my energy for the nerve-racking night mass air refueling and the arduous flight across the Atlantic. When you're strapped in an ejection seat for 11 hours, it can be quite a chore. Unlike an airliner, there is no place to go in a B-47. You just sit there and take it.

Harry broke my concentration, and I jumped, involuntarily. "We're not closing on the lead. Air refueling descent point in 25 miles. I have the others at that point, now." I disengaged the autopilot and retrimmed the aircraft.

"Can you read the tanker beacon signals, Harry?" The B-47 radar has the capability of "painting" electronic beacon signals through special circuits.

"They're out there, but the signals are not well defined, yet."

"Roger, We'll go in on our own. At least they got off the ground at Goose Bay."

"Olive flight, this is lead. Standby for descent in five seconds. Do you read, Olive 4?"

"Roger, lead. We're coming in about four minutes behind you on our radar. We'll make it."

"Understand, Olive 4. Go in on your own."

We started down and accelerated to maintain 315 knots. "Harry, lock onto No. 4 tanker if you can, and keep giving me range and bearings at 10 mile intervals until 10 miles, then every mile from the tanker."

"Roger. Tankers are at 70 miles, 5 degrees right. We're eight miles behind the others."

"60 miles, 2 degrees right." I corrected, and maintained my speed.

"50 miles, dead ahead." I maintained my heading, descent and speed.

"40 miles, same heading. No. 4 is 2 degrees right." I made a slight heading correction. We experienced a mild amount of turbulence, but nothing to get worried about. The Prowlers, wings flapped, but we felt nothing in the cockpit.

Bob broke in and he sounded excited. "Dave, there's a fighter at 10 o'clock low. He's on a pursuit curve towards the tankers. Watch out for him. I don't know if he knows we're here." That must have shaken Harry, for he also saw the fighter on his radar. The blip suddenly appeared out of nowhere, and he muttered to no one in particular. I glanced into the black night, and ahead, to the left and below us, was our unwelcome guest, wing lights blinking, on his way towards the tankers.

"I have him. He must be crazy, horsing around all these birds. I hope he knows what he's doing." That's all we need, I thought.

"Olive flight, this is lead. If you have your tanker, take over on individual rendezvous." I confirmed and told Bob, "Go to our refueling frequency, Harry?"

"Range 15 miles, dead ahead. Maintain present heading. His signal is strong and clear." We were four miles behind the others.

"Ann 54, this is Olive 4, do you read?"

"Roger, Olive 4. We have you at 10 miles, on course. Our altitude is 17,500, airspeed 200. We have 50,000 pounds available. Glad you could make it." We'd need it after consuming extra fuel in our high speed chase.

"Range 10 miles, course good." I leveled the aircraft at 17,000 feet, and kept the airspeed at 280 knots. The receiver (bomber) levels off 500 feet below the tanker altitude to provide safe separation between the two aircraft until the receiver sights the tanker and is within two miles of him.

"Air refueling check, Bob." I transferred control of the fuel panel to Bob's crew position so he could direct fuel into specific tanks to maintain proper center of gravity, which is critical at heavy aircraft weights.

Finishing the checklist, he advised, "Three mains open, bomb bay open, forward and aft aux. open. Standing by the refueling door." Bob purposely left the wing tank valves closed, for they were full, and any fuel we could get into the lines to those tanks would be negligible.

* * * *

Air refueling is an experience that no one forgets once he has gone through it. Each time it becomes a personal challenge, man versus machine, the individual versus time, the elements versus physical dexterity. The technique for a successful mid-air refueling contradicts every concept of coordinated flight. Normally, when making a turn you drop the wing (using ailerons), add back pressure on the control column (when in a turn the wings lose their lift and the nose tends to drop), add rudder (to get the nose to turn), and add a little power (to counteract the loss of lift). Level turns are a smooth, coordinated maneuver, using the flight instruments to help you.

Refueling is totally different in both concept and action. Moving 170,000 pounds a maximum of five feet is the problem that confronts the pilot. The stability of the tanker is a great assist; his instability magnifies the receivers positioning problem. A good tanker pilot will not "fight" weather-caused instability, rather he will "ride" out the temporary changes in his aircraft attitude. This the receiver pilot can cope with, but when the tanker changes his "platform" because of temporary attitude change, the bomber pilot really has a tremendous problem. An experienced bomber pilot can tell, after a few minutes, if the tanker pilot is an "old hand" or not.

Teaching air refueling is unlike anything any bomber flight instructor has experienced. A good refueling pilot doesn't mean he can instruct refueling to a novice pilot. The communication between instructor and pilot is a matter of personal effectiveness, non-standard in that each pilot reacts differently in an air refueling situation. It's not like teaching a pilot to fly, whether it be visual flight or on instruments. Refueling is more reaction than action. There is absolutely no way to tell who is going to be a good refueler and who is not, based on his previous experience. Of the many I've instructed in refueling, I found it prudent to ignore past experience and flying time and concentrate on individual reaction. Small or tall, fat or thin, it is impossible to foretell if a otherwise-qualified pilot can be a successful bomber refueling pilot. I've had pilots with 5,000 flying hours unable to refuel, even after 11 or 12 instructional rides (six was the authorized number in the curriculum). Conversely, some make it after three or four flights. With all those I instructed, only three could make contact and hold it on the first flight, and they were former fighter pilots. One of them was a full colonel, Dave Schilling, a celebrated World War II fighter ace attached to us to learn the bomber business. Ironically enough, he was one of the easiest to teach.

Many pilots fly mechanically, rather than by instinct, or "by the seat of their pants." The lack of flexibility, that of "unlearning" what has been drummed in one's head in teaching coordinated flight, was the downfall of many a prospective SAC bomber pilot. Many otherwise good pilots couldn't bridge the gap. Maybe the inflexibility aspect is the reason the majority of service academy graduates had a lot of trouble. It's unfortunate, but every combat mission profile included at least one refueling, and, if you couldn't get your fuel you couldn't get to the target and back. It was just that simple. Because the responsibility to determine the qualification of a pilot was a great one, each pilot was tutored by at least two instructors during his checkout flights. Marginal pilots were given extra instruction before they were allowed to take their final check ride by the Wing Standardization Section.

No amount of ground instruction can prepare the neophyte for what is in store for him on his first refueling instructional flight. One person can't tell another's muscles when and how to react to controlling a 80-ton aircraft within such restrictive parameters. The approach to the tanker and boom is the same as formation flying, but there it stops. The pilot must be able to maneuver in six directions, at least three simultaneously. If you approach a stationary object slowly, then you only have to worry about the fore-and-aft movement, controlled by the throttles. If you drift to the left, now the aircraft must be moved to the right, and here's where the problem starts. You must slide to the right, which calls for cross-controlling, or right rudder and left aileron, but it must be done with precision and speed, and only momentarily. If the pilot holds the correction, he will overcorrect every time, then he will have to correct in the opposite direction. Let the aircraft drop too low and you have to raise the nose and add power. As the correction takes affect, the pilot must reduce power and release the back pressure on the control column. All of these

things can happen at once, and, when you consider tanker instability or rough air, the bomber pilots' problems magnify corre-
spondingly. As to the mounting problems, the additional weight
of the fuel onloaded by the receiver, and this requires both additional power and trim, it can be readily seen any refueling is always physically and psychologically exhausting. The mental an-
guish caused by wanting to do the job can, and does, cause tense-
ness and this complicates the physical reactions so necessary to
"muscle the monster" around the sky.

Practice, practice and more practice is the key to continued
success in aerial refueling once it is established you can do it.
There used to be a "standby" tanker flying in the local area any-
time a B-47 was in the air (in case an emergency required it; in
the early years the B-47 had a lot of gear problems, necessitating
low altitude flying, often beyond the fuel capacity of the bird),
and we used him every opportunity we got. Most refueling is
done with the tanker maintaining the same heading throughout
the refueling. If a turn is required (for weather or to stay inside
the designated area) it was made at only a 10 degree bank angle.
To keep ourselves sharp, we had a quasi-illegal maneuver that
went like this: make contact and have the tanker start a 10 degree
bank, then increase it to 20 degrees, then increase it to 30 degrees, while still maintaining contact. Holding contact in a 30
degree bank really requires concentration, reaction and technique.
Now, after the tanker has held his bank through a 180 degree
turn, you tell him to reverse his bank, ending up in a 30 degree
bank in the opposite direction, all the time maintaining contact.
Thinking this maneuver through, the reader will realize that it is
the zenith of accuracy for a refueling pilot. In our experience,
only one out of a hundred qualified pilots could do it successfully. The first time we did it, there were three of us instructors
flying together to maintain our instructor proficiency. The tanker
pilot couldn't believe what he and we did. It had never been done
before and most pilots wouldn't even attempt it. Tex was with
me and said he'd try anything once and did. Jack, the long-time

SAC pilot, was along and had his serious doubts that it was being done, but after Tex and I went through the maneuver, he figured he better give it a try and did. The tanker pilot made it a point to examine our sanity after we landed. He finally walked away, muttering to himself. Ah, life can be fun, even in SAC.

As I have said, refueling to maximum onload normally takes a 20-40 minute contact. It doesn't sound like much, but consider trying to drive you car over the Bay Bridge between Oakland and San Francisco (eight miles) with your left front wheel on the dividing line, all the way.

Now that the uninitiated (an apt phrase, if you think about it) begins to see what confronts a pilot about to take on fuel, let's add one more obstacle, darkness. During daylight operations, the horizon can sometimes be used as a positioning reference, as can the wings of the tanker. Likewise, the approach to the "envelope" is fairly easy during the daytime for gauging distances. At night it's a whole new ball game. First of all, it's almost impossible to determine distances at night, so the pilot relies solely on radar and must follow a precise speed schedule until a half mile separates the two planes. Overrunning the tanker is the big hazard of night rendezvous. Once the approach has been completed, and you're entering the envelope, you can distinctly see the boom lites, the pilot director lites and the tanker engine exhausts. The outline of the tanker is indistinct and there is no horizon for reference. All this time the pilot must maintain strict visual contact with the tanker and cannot divert his attention to his instruments, so he has no way of knowing if he is in level flight. The horizon reference is critical. The director lights are of no use until contact is made. Once in position for contact, the biggest hazard is to keep from staring at the boom. Remember that the pilot is now flying strictly by "feel" 20 feet from another aircraft.

The first time the boom slams into the bomber receptacle at night, the psychological shock is almost overpowering. There you are, less than 20 feet from another aircraft, and are now joined by an inflexible umbilical staring at you. Your movements are strictly instinctive. Reduce power, back on the controls, right rudder, left aileron, nudge the power forward, eyes moving all the time. Watch the director lights, look at the boom, align yourself with the body of the tanker, change trim as you take on fuel, more power, trim, and on and on. Time seems to stand still. The boom operator talks to you, your copilot tells you about fuel distribution, radar advises of "time to go," and all of your senses are working overtime. Your nerves are taut, your eyeballs ache, your back and arm muscles tighten, and you feel as if its never going to end. Your mind is concentrating on the task at hand; you block out any other thoughts for you know that you can't let any outside influences interrupt the instinctive reactions vitally necessary to "hang in there."

When the final signal is given to disconnect, the whole thing seems unreal, but the mechanical responses continue. Punch the "disconnect" button, throttle back, hold altitude, wait, watch the tanker accelerate (from the black smoke that comes from his exhausts) and climb ahead, add power, accelerate, move straight ahead, and only then does your mind release its hold on your actions, and you can begin to think again. Almost immediately you feel the weariness take effect, the physical, mental and psychological fatigue that has been unconsciously building up. It is almost like a water tap being opened.

You are drained, and only now does your brain start recalling the events. Air refueling is a form of self hypnosis, and anyone who has gone through this process never ceases to be amazed how he can block out everything but a single purpose, that of successfully overcoming one of the most unnatural feats of airmanship. It is a rewarding effort and not easily forgotten.

* * * *

"Range four miles, dead ahead." I immediately chopped the power to idle, trimmed the aircraft and said, "Bob, give me the airspeed each mile."

"Three miles."

"Airspeed 250 knots."

"Two miles."

"Airspeed 240 knots."

I looked ahead and saw all four tankers stepped down to the right. Ours was dead ahead, low man in the formations. The other bombers were already in the refueling position.

"Bob, open the door." There was a sudden sound of rushing air, slowing us even more, as the air refueling door opened into the slipstream. I started a gradual climb to the refueling envelope. As the door locked open, the green "ready for contact" light illuminated on the upper left of my instrument panel, meaning we had all the switches and circuits in the proper position to take on fuel.

"Olive 4, this is Ann 54 boomer. Have you visual, ready for contact."

"Roger, boom, Olive 4 ready for contact. All tanks open. Request full pressure." I was still trying to catch up on our timing.

"Roger, Olive 4. Forward 25 (feet), up 10(feet). Standby for contact. Thought for a minute you weren't going to show up."

We were sliding into position, the boom and boom lights dead ahead. I maneuvered forward and up, ever closer, closer, wham.

"Contact, 54."

"Contact, Olive 4."

"Dave, that fighter is still around. He's ahead and to the right, looks like he's making a pass at us," Harry announced. Out of the corner of my eye, I saw the wing lights as he came barreling through and under the formation. I'd bet he had his hands full. "Roger, Harry. He just went between three and four on our left. Hope he's having fun." He's playing a dangerous game, I thought.

The director lights, on the belly of the tanker, showed green, or that I was in the right position. The lights could show aft, forward, up and down, indicating the correction to be made, if you weren't in the "slot."

"Stabilized at 200 knots. We're taking on fuel," Bob advised, as we increased our weight because of the added fuel. When this occurred, adding power and retrimming the aircraft was necessary, on a continuing basis. For every 10,000 pounds offloaded by the tanker, he automatically increased his speed by 10 knots, to offset the additional speed needed by the B-47 to maintain adequate control because of the increased weight.

"Airspeed 210. We've taken on 10,000 pounds, 20 minutes to disconnect." Bob kept me informed as we took on each 10,000 pounds, so I could gauge our performance.

Refueling inflight is physical torture. Reactions must be immediate, instantaneous, and movements positive. Once you get a disconnect, you've got to work twice as hard to get back into position, and precious time and fuel are lost. Fortunately, this was going well. The tanker pilot was holding a nice, smooth platform.

"Airspeed 220, you have 30,000 pounds, 10 minutes to the end of AR (air refueling). Our timing is good; we're only about a minute behind schedule." Although the cabin temperature was turned way down, I was sweating, the moisture running down into the bottom of my oxygen mask. As the weight was nearing the critical condition, the controls were losing some of their responsiveness, and holding position was getting more difficult. I couldn't afford the luxury of releasing the throttles to empty the pooled sweat, so I just sweated it out. I would have a raw chin tomorrow.

"Olive 4, you have the scheduled onload. Will continue to transfer fuel until the end of AR."

"Roger, boom. That's fine. We'll hang on until our time is up."

"Five minutes to disconnect," Harry advised. New course will be 085." Close and continuous coordination is the key to any successful crews' performance, but crews who know when to do something have the edge. We were a close-knit trio and I was never more proud of them than I was during each refueling. They always knew when to say something that took some of the pressure off of me.

"Olive 4, Ann 54," the tanker navigator broke in. "Eng AR. Disconnect, now."

I punched the disconnect button on the left handle of the control column, reduced power, and dropped down, all in one movement. The tanker simultaneously added power and climbed straight ahead. Bob located the other three receivers. "The other three are to the left and ahead," he said. I added 100% power on all six engines, let the aircraft accelerate to 280 knots, then raised the nose to maintain that speed.

"Olive 4, this is Ann 54, 45,000 pounds transferred, one contact. You sure made it look easy. Good luck. Cleared to interplane frequency."

"Roger, 54. Thanks. Good platform. Good luck getting back home." He was going to have trouble landing at Goose Bay.

Bob changed frequencies and called Olive lead. As I maneuvered to get into loose formation once again, the leader called. "Olive flight, this is Lead. Good refueling. Coast out at 32. Level off at 330. Glad to have you with us, Four." It was now 2120 (9:20 p.m.).

"Coast out point 50 miles, 10 degrees left," Harry offered. "Bob, we'll take our first shot at 45, our precomp will work out OK." There's Harry and his preplanning, again.

"Roger on first shot. We're 4,000 pounds above the line. I'm going to turn around, now." Bob was saying we have 4,000 pounds more than predicted on our fuel curve prediction, even though we had used excessive power settings to catch up with the flight. Good show. That extra fuel was the difference from what we got from the tanker and what we were scheduled to receive. Now Bob was getting ready to take sightings on the stars, putting in his ejection seat pins, and rotate the seat so he had more freedom to use the sextant. The B-47 had a porthole in the top of the plastic canopy where the periscopic sextant fitted over the copilot's head.

"Olive flight, this is lead. Over departure point at 32. Proceeding on heading 075. Check in with me every 30 minutes."

"AC, this is Nav. Heading 075 looks good. I've got a good radar fix for departure on our nav leg. Bob, we'll shoot as planned. First shot at 45, Dube; second shot at 48, Canopus; third shot at 51, Deneb. I'll hack you when to start."

Bob had the same set of figures as Harry, but neither one of them left anything to chance. Bob had a navigator watch to check his timing, but we always used Harry's watch for it was from his watch we based our timing. Now all I had to do was monitor the stability of the plane, transfer fuel, and make the radio reports. I really had nothing to do until Harry and Bob finished their three-star fix, except plot their celestial fixes on my map, and try to get radio bearings to verify our position.

* * * *

We were an hour east of the coast of Canada and three cups of coffee later. I'd checked in with Olive Leader and was now about to contact Ocean Station Bravo. The overseas radio facility charts showed the location of each Navy ship permanently stationed in the Atlantic for navigation assistance and rescue support, if necessary.

"Ocean Station Bravo, this is Spiral Olive 4, over." They're supposed to monitor specific radio frequencies at all times, but sometimes you have to call four or five times, and sometimes they just don't answer at all.

"Roger, Spiral Olive 4, this is Bravo. Can we be of assistance?" Will wonders never cease? He answered after the third try.

"Bravo, this is Olive 4. Request position. Will transmit tone for 60 seconds, over."

"Roger, Four. Go ahead." As I depressed the tone button, I could hear the steady humming noise in my earphones.

"Harry, I'll have a position for you in a minute." "OK, I'll take a shot on Polaris. That should give us a good course line," he answered.

"Olive 4, this is Station Bravo. We are Kilo 5. Have you 52 miles, bearing 350 magnetic. Class 4 fix, over."

"Roger, Bravo. Thank you. How's the weather down there?" "Not bad, but it's cold and choppy, but the coffee's hot. Have a good flight. Out."

Each ocean station must remain within 60 miles of its published location. Kilo 5 meant he was 12 miles southeast of that location, and we were 56 miles almost due north of him. The accuracy of his fix was good. He measures this on a scale of one to five, one being poor and five being excellent.

"AC, this is Nav. Plotted our position, and he's 10 miles off, but that's close enough. Our ground speeds' now 585 knots. We're near the forecasted jet stream. In one minute turn left to 065." As I corrected the heading, I realized the jet stream was stronger than forecasted, and Harry was compensating for it. He lets us maintain the initial course for over an hour, then, based on his fixes, establishes a new course. He knows exactly what he's doing, and both Bob and I have implicit faith in his ability.

We'd been flying for over five hours, endless cups of coffee and a flight lunch later, we were about to coast-in at Prestwick, Scotland. Harry's final correction was over 30 minutes ago and we were going to hit it right on the nose. He did it again. I could see Prestwick lights ahead and the radio beacon verified it. The Prestwick Beacon was a high powered radio transmitter and could be picked up on our receiver at least 500 miles away. The transatlantic commercial flights used it extensively.

"Olive Flight, this is Lead. Estimating Prestwick at 05. Turn on individual flight plans. Present weather at Heyford is 800 overcast, two miles in fog and smoke. No change for two hours. Everyone check in. Over." All of the flight checked in on bomber common frequency. So far so good. We hadn't lost anybody.

We had an hour and a half to go, so we shouldn't have a problem with weather on landing, if the forecast held good.

Chapter 18

STRIKE AGAINST LAROCHELLE

"AC, this is Nav. Over Prestwick at 04. ETA (Estimated Time of Arrival) was 30 seconds off. New heading 150; 45 minutes to IP."

"You're slipping, Harry. Must be your clock," I chided. Any time your estimate is within five minutes of your actual time of arrival, especially after five hours of no landmark, is considered excellent. Harry didn't have time to savor his good fortune, for now he was putting his celestial data away, tuning up his radar, and studying the target charts.

"AC, this is pilot. Rotating and strapping in. Ejection pins out. Fuel panel looks good. Transfer must have gone OK. We're 6,000 pounds above the line. Radar, standing by pre-bombing checklist."

"Crew, this is AC. Climbing to 39,000. Heading now is 150." Our flight plan called for a change in altitude at this point.

As we steadied on our new course and altitude, I could see London in the distance, its lights blossoming through the overcast. Large cities cast an eerie glow through cloud cover, with no distinct impression of shapes, just a wide expanse of illumination. It's a beautiful sight and I never grow weary of seeing the display at night.

"Unidentified aircraft at 2 o'clock, low, moving fast," Bob exclaimed. I looked below and to my right, and, sure enough, there was an airplane coming up towards us.

"Got him, Bob. Get on the guns. See if you can pick him up." At our altitude and speed, a fighter could only attack from the rear, where our radar-controlled guns would protect us. The guns were not loaded, but we had to react to any attack, for practice.

Bob didn't answer, but I could see him turning around to his radar set, located on the rear bulkhead of the crew compartment.

"Roger, Dave. Set's on and I have him three miles, 1,000 feet below. He's holding steady, not gaining." I smiled to myself. One thing about the B-47, no fighter could keep up with us unless he was already above us. This was one honey of an aircraft.

"He's falling back to four miles. He won't give up. Maybe our speed surprises him," Bob mused. "I'm going to lose him at this rate." The range of the B-47's gunnery is accurate up to 10 miles, and extremely accurate within seven miles.

"He's broken off. Dropped below my set's range, but going straight below us." I caught a glimpse of his wing lights as he moved off and entered into the overcast. Our position was northeast of London, so he must have been a RAF Defense Night Fighter.

"AC, turn right to 195. Cherbourg ahead, 30 miles, ETA Pre-IP at 30. At 30 accelerate to 460 knots," Harry advised.

We normally cruise at 425 knots true airspeed, but our USCM bomb runs were made at a higher speed. The B-47 could fly a lot faster than that, but was limited because of possible structural damage to the wing tanks over a sustained time at higher speeds. If an actual war existed, we would drop the wing tanks when they were empty.

Over Cherbourg, I turned left to 180 degrees, pushed the throttles up to 98% RPM, and Bob started the Bomb Run Checklist.

"450, 455, 460 knots. Hold her there, Dave," Harry said. I moved the throttles back to 94% to maintain the present speed and adjusted the trim. Our ground speed was now over 650 miles per hour.

"Over the IP. Turn left to 170. 1 have the target under the crosshairs. Give me control." I turned the control switch to "remote."

"Your aircraft. Three minutes on the timer." The radar operator could now control the aircraft through his radar controls. Now all I had to do is call of the "time-to-go" to Harry to cross-check his timing.

"Checking No. 1 offset. OK. Checking No. 2 offset. OK. Going back to primary."

"Roger, 180 seconds to go."

"Bombing checklist complete," Bob finalized.

"Roger, target's breaking up. She's looking good. I've got the aiming point. We're really moving. Wind is 290 degrees at 170 knots," Harry advised, looking at his wind dials, which were visual displays of his radar interpretation.

"Roger. 45 seconds. Bob, standby for breakaway turn to the left."

"Roger, you're clear to the left."

"10 seconds, - 5 seconds, - BOMBS AWAY!"

The red "bombs away light" on my instrument panel blinked, confirming the simulated bomb release point. I punched the autopilot disconnect button, racked the B-47 into a 45 degree bank, fought to keep the nose from dropping, felt the control surfaces buffeting near a high speed stall, and kept the turn going just below the buffeting angle.

"Five seconds to roll-out," Bob counted. "Roll out, NOW," he said, as I slowly eased the bird back onto an even keel. This maneuver is designed to get the plane away from the shock wave of an atomic blast, and we practiced every chance we got. Turn too far and you head to the full effect of the blast, too shallow a turn and you won't get far enough away. It's a pretty violent maneuver and you have to wrestle the flight controls all the time in the turn.

"Post release check complete. Turn left to 005. Good breakaway. Upper Heyford at 55. We would have been out of the critical blast area," Harry noted. "The railroad yards at La Rochelle are theoretically no longer there. Radar photography will confirm a good run." He obviously was happy with the radar run.

Established on the new heading, I reduced the airspeed back to 425 knots, trimmed the aircraft, engaged the autopilot, and got out the letdown chart for Upper Heyford from the chart case by my right leg.

"Bob, let's review the let-down. Monitor the instruments while I look it over. Harry, when we're in range, put the cross-hairs on the runway. "Each major airfield has established let-down procedures, minimum weather ceiling and visibility, obstructions and airfield layout. Although Bob and I had flown into Upper Heyford before, we also went through the approach in the simulator trainer at Lake Charles as had every AC and pilot.

Over Cherbourg, I turned on the inbound leg to Upper Heyford, and started our extensive communication's procedure to get us on the ground.

"London Center, this is Spiral Olive 4. Over Cherbourg at 41, Flight level 390. Request present weather at Heyford and clearance to Approach Control."

"Roger, Olive 4. Squak ident. Over." London Radar was confirming our position. Our IFF (Indentification-Friend-Or-Foe) electronic set when activated caused our radar image to "bloom" on the ground radar scope. They had our position, based on our flight plan estimate and this procedure would pinpoint us.

"Olive 4, we have you in positive radar contact. Present Heyford weather is 800 feet overcast, two miles in fog and drizzle. Cleared to descend to and maintain Flight Level 220 (22,000 ft). No other traffic. Contact approach control, now."

"Dave, I've got the base under the crosshairs. Center the PDI (Pilots Direction Indicator). You're 90 miles out. I turned five degrees right to center the PDI, reduced power and started down from 39,000 feet.

"Bob, you've got the radios. Give 'em a call." From now on Bob would handle the radio calls, leaving me free to concentrate on flying the approach.

"Heyford approach, this is Spiral Olive 4, passing flight level 300, for flight level 220."

"Olive 4, this is Heyford Approach. We have you 70 miles south. Continue descent to 10,000 feet. This will be a straight-in approach to runway 30. Altimeter 29.87. Call through flight level 200, and reaching 10,000. You are number one for approach." Bob acknowledged and down we went.

"Bob, drag gear (rear main landing gear and outriggers) coming down. Start the Before Landing Check." The B-47 is so aerodynamically clean that the airspeed builds up amazingly fast in a descent, even with the power in idle. To keep the speed down, you have to reduce the angle of descent (which will extend the distance traveled, putting the aircraft too close to the landing runway), or lower the gear. Gear down caused a lot of vibration during the descent, but she really comes down like an express elevator with the "garbage" out. The drag gear came down, and indicated "down and locked" on the instrument panels. We keep the forward main up until the landing pattern is reached because of the speed limitation (195 knots) on the forward gear doors.

"Approach, this is Olive 4. Approaching 10,000 feet."

"Roger, Olive 4. Continue your descent and maintain 4,000 feet. You are 20 miles out. Turn right to 345." We were now traveling about four miles per minute over the ground. I eased my descent, to bleed off some of the excess airspeed.

"Dave, they're angling you in to the runway. Disregard the PDI unless you lose radio contact," Harry suggested. He had a copy of the letdown in front of him and was following the entire procedure and would standby the entire approach in case I needed help. We completed the "before landing check" and slowed to approach speed. We broke out at 600 feet, right on centerline. I switched on the landing lights. The runway looked awfully short (8,000 feet) and narrow (100 feet wide, versus 200 feet wide that we were used to at Lake Charles). Most of the runways we used were 10,000 feet long. The B-47 bases had their original runways lengthened to accommodate the landing requirements of heavy jet bombers. The B-52s aren't any better.

Landing at night at a strange field requires a different technique that setting her down at a base you're used to. The approach speed is designed to be 20 knots above stalling; when you change the aircraft attitude from approach to landing attitude, 10 knots are lost, and that gives you 10 knots to "bleed off," hence the longer landing roll. When landing at a base with a shorter runway, you must necessarily "drag" the aircraft in, meaning a longer, flatter approach, using more power because the B-47 is in a landing attitude when you come in low and flat. In this configuration, reducing the power to idle allows the aircraft to touch-down almost immediately, whereas under a normal approach the B-47 will float about 1500 feet down the runway from where you "round out."

As I approached the runway threshhold, the runway was intermittently obscured by a fine drizzle and patchy fog. I had the Prowler trimmed properly for such an approach and the airspeed was right on the money, so I continued on. The fog dissipated as I crossed the approach lights, and I was able to set her down about 200 from the runway end, pulled the chute, braked slowly, and let her roll to slow speed to the far end, turning off at the last taxiway with no problem. Bob switched to ground control.

"Upper Heyford ground, this is Spiral Olive 4, clearing the runway. Chute gone. Standing by for taxi instructions." Ground control cleared us to the ramp, and we followed the parking vehicle. We were soon nestled between two of the squadrons aircraft. Being the last aircraft to land, things were quiet and there was none of the hustle and bustle when one was landing, one was taxiing and one was parking. We shut down the engines and aircraft systems, and the effects of the long flight crept over us.

The quiet blended with the gloom of a foggy morning.

"Welcome to England," said Si, our Squadron CO, as we wearily climbed down. "The bus will take you to the mess hall and then to your quarters. The Old Man wants us all together at the briefing room at 11 o'clock. Hell of a good job, Dave. I know you can use a few days off, but he'll explain what's going on at the meeting. I've got to run," and off he went in his jeep, leaving us to unload our gear. If I knew Si, and I did, he was hurrying to a party. He never missed a chance to "bend the elbow."

"Vince, stay close to the maintenance shack until you hear what's planned for us," I cautioned our crew chief, still groggy from the long hours of sitting. He nodded, grabbed his gear and went to talk to the line chief in the maintenance van. We had been cramped in our seats for almost nine hours. In review, the flight from the U.S. was almost routine, after the hectic second takeoff attempt and the chase to air refueling. We were all tired but satisfied we had done our job. The long overwater portion of the flight had gone without a hitch, and Harry had brought us right "down the pipe" on our landfall. We had had a good bomb run, the emergency breakaway maneuver was satisfactory and the landing was under control. We had packed one hell of a lot of activity and training in almost nine hours actual flying time.

From my personal standpoint, the night air refueling was the most satisfying. No matter how many times I did it at night, I always got a thrill out of seeing the flight of tankers ahead during an approach, their green, red and white lights blinking in the black darkness. Other than the lead aircraft, the No. 4 bomber (in a four-plane formation) had the easiest time, because he wasn't sandwiched in between others, and he didn't have to fight prop wash by being on the outside. I will always remember the practice night mass refueling we did out in the Gulf of Mexico. I was No. 3 in a five-plane formation, which meant I had two on my left going after their tankers, and two on my right doing the same thing. As we leveled out five miles behind the tankers, I could see all five of them strung out left and right. Counting from the left, I picked out mine and bored in on him. Out of the corner of my eye I could see another B-47 charge past me and into my line of approach. My plane got caught in his jet wash and we almost flipped over. At about three miles he realized his mistake and slid back to the left to his own tanker. About this time my copilot yelled that was a B-47 coming in from the right. I hurriedly glanced up and saw him. He was going after my tanker. Certainly a popular fellow. Going at 300 miles per hour, at night, is no way to play a game of "who's got whose tanker," and I slid over and took the No. 4 tanker. I wasn't about to argue with anybody that night and under those conditions.

Fortunately, everything turned out without mishap, but I had a few well-chosen words to both AC's. It was almost comical, because we were flying in a mixed formation, which meant crews from all three squadrons were in the formation. The one who cut me off first was the Squadron Operations Officer of the 66th and he couldn't believe what he had done. He was an old timer at the game. It took the tanker AC to straighten him out, and then, reluctantly, he saw what he had done. We were good friends and joked about the fiasco, afterwards.

Unfortunately for him, he was flying that night to maintain his proficiency, not having a crew of his own.

The other clown was a different matter. The second one to cut me off was the 68th Squadron CO, with an instructor riding in the copilots' seat. He, too, was "keeping his hand in," so to speak. When I approached him, and I must admit none too tactfully, he was outraged that I would accuse him of "such a flagrant violation of air safety," as he indignantly put it. He wouldn't discuss the matter with me any further, so I looked up the Instructor Pilot who had been flying with him, and he readily admitted the CO had screwed up, but he wasn't about to talk to him about it. I thought that was the end of it, but when the mission accomplishment forms, a detailed outline of what our crew had accomplished on the flight, hit the Wing Training Office, it was obvious that someone had refueled with the wrong tanker. The tanker crews saw what had happened and the pompous one had his rear-end chewed by the Wing DO. It didn't do much good, I'm afraid, for the poacher ended up as the new DO, and his personal image of himself only got worse.

The ride in the minibus to the Quarters was a hassle in itself. The British driver obviously wanted to get back to the sanctuary of his warm motor pool office, for he careened through the streets of the base, and deposited us, somewhat shaken out of our lethargy, in front of the combination mess and quarters. The building was a two-story affair, quite old, ivy-covered, with a large portico and a stone entranceway. Inside it looked almost like an old-fashioned hotel, and the NCO assigned us to a large room on the second floor. He indicated the mess was being held open for us, and the cooks would appreciate it if we could finish our meal in the next 30 minutes, for they had been on duty for 10 hours. I felt like telling him it was a pity we were holding them up, caused by our late arrival, but I wasn't in any mood to badger him. Besides, the thought of good hot food had its usual calming affect. Someone once said there are those who eat to live, and then there are those who live to eat, and I've never been criticized as a light eater.

Four eggs, plenty of sausage and toast, canned orange juice and plenty of coffee helped to ease the weariness of the flight. Even better was the ensuing, leisurely hot shower, and best yet was the crisp clean sheets and all three of us conked out, knowing we would get about six hours sleep, and then be rudely awakened by the charge of quarters airman, telling us it was time to get up.

Chapter 19

England, Rest and Recuperation

"Come on you guys, the bus is waiting. We'll miss the train." Tex was ready to go, and he had organized a group party to go to London, and "bust the place apart," to use his words. Bob was frantically jamming clothes into his hand bag, and ran for the bus.

"Bob, remember what the Old Man said. I can fly the beast by myself, but I sure as hell don't want to have to explain to Laverne why you had to stay over in England," I admonished, as he disappeared down the stairs, waving as he leaped into the bus.

Harry was lying on his bed, smiling. He was remembering how we had to hastily drag Bob from the bar in Casablanca, after he had challenged a monstrous British infantry captain to a "knock-down, drag-out" fight, just because the "glorious" reputation of Texas had been impugned in his eyes. It was quite comical. Bob was five feet five inches tall and weighs about 120 pounds, wringing wet. The Britisher was over six feet and at least 190 pounds. It would have been a slaughter if the MPs hadn't arrived and rounded up some other rowdies. Fortunately, Harry spotted the rear exit, and we both manhandled Bob away from there, vigorously flailing his arms and vocally protesting the treatment he was getting. Bob is very quiet when sober, but hard liquor makes him "eight feet tall and ready to take on the world" if his native state isn't revered in the same light as he sees it.

"Let's go down to the snack bar and get something to eat," Harry suggested. Although we ate at 3:00 a.m., had coffee and doughnuts at the briefing at 11:00 a.m., both of us were ready for a good, leisurely meal. We hadn't planned anything special to do on our three days off, so we were going to take our time, and maybe something would come up that was interesting.

The earlier briefing by the Wing CO was sketchy, but told us we had three days off before we could expect to get back to work and ready ourselves for the unannounced strike against the U.S. The Colonel cautioned us of three things: everyone to be back by 8:00 p.m. on the third day, don't get into trouble, and don't discuss our forthcoming mission. "Remember, Security Service will be around, and I damned sure don't want anyone in my outfit up on charges for having a big mouth," he cautioned. "I'm turning you animals loose on the poor English, but try to remember they are our allies, so act like human beings for a change." Nice parting thought.

* * * *

"Let's walk, Harry. We need to stretch our legs and get the circulation going." The fog and clouds had burned off, and the sun was warming on our backs as we made our way to the base snack bar. After the long haul last night, it took me about 12 hours to get my system back into its normal routine. This was long before "jet lag" became a popular phrase. The time difference (four hours) caused most of us to have difficulty acclimating ourselves after these missions. A 10 minute walk would help.

"Why don't we take the bus down to the Regional Exchange this afternoon?" Harry suggested. "We could pick up some Christmas presents. I heard they also have embroidered wings real cheap." The English artisans do a magnificent job of embroidering flight insignia by hand, using silver thread. They look beautiful on the uniform.

We arrived at the Snack Bar about 1:00 p.m. and the lunch crowd had disappeared, so we didn't have to wait for our meal. During the leisurely brunch, we decided to catch the 2:00 p.m. bus, which would deliver us at the Exchange at 3:00. There was a shuttle transportation every two hours for the convenience of Air Force personnel at the various installations within 100 miles. The local base exchanges in England only stocked the bare necessities, whereas the Regional Exchange carried a wide variety of items.

* * * *

The bus ride was like a tonic, for I have always loved the English countryside. The ancient-looking brick homes, the narrow quaint cobblestone streets, the ever present bicycle riders, the colorful signs, all touched me deeply, as they had in 1943 when I had flown B-17s for the Eighth Air Force over Germany, been shot down by fighters, captured, escaped, and made my way to Sweden. I was flown back to my unit in England in a RAF Mosquito, where I completed my tour of combat duty.

Harry and I had little to say to one another. We were just enjoying the scenery. Neither of us felt the need to talk.

The trip back was just as pleasant as the trip down. We both had made several purchases, and, all in all, were a happy pair. When we arrived at Heyford, Harry got off at the BOQ and I continued on the bus to the Command Post. While we were at Heyford, we had a staff duty officer in the local Command Post all the time. Once the security guard identified me by my flight line badge and checked off my name as one of those allowed entry into the "inner sanctum," I entered the darkened room, noted two duty controllers at the communications console and our duty officer at his own desk. Sully (Maj. Sullivan) was a casual friend, having flown with us several times. "What can I do for you, Dave?" "Do you have the flight plan for Texas League available?" Knowing what I had in mind, he reached in a file drawer and pulled out our crew folder, saying I could use the conference room if I wanted to.

"Thanks, Sully. I thought Harry and I would start to work, so we can have plenty of time."

"You bet. It doesn't look good for the 5th of December. The tankers had a hell of a time getting back in after refueling you guys coming over, and it doesn't look like they can get off, and there's no alternate for them to use. SAC still says we 'go' on the fifth but weather says 'no.' The Old Man has been calling in from London every two hours, but he doesn't think SAC can afford to have all of us here for an extended period of time."

"OK. I'll fill out the flight plan and set up the maps, but leave the winds out. At least we can get that much done. I'll sign out the folder and store it in my briefcase if that's OK with you." He had no objection, for we left our briefcases in the secured command post. I signed for the classified crew folder, read over the operations order, filled out our flight log, annotated my maps, then put the paperwork in my flight bag and left it with Sully. He was about to say something, but the phone rang and he waved me off. I caught the bus back to our quarters. Harry was back in our room taking a nap. He opened his eyes as I closed the door and looked at his watch. "Where have you been all this time, chasing the WAFS?" I looked at my watch and was surprised that I had been in the CP for almost two hours. "I wish I had. Unfortunately, I only laid out the flight plan for Texas League. Looks like 12 hours. The weather stinks at Harmon, Goose, Iceland and Greenland. Could be one hell of a refueling. Sully seems to think there will be a delay."

"Twelve hours! My God, that's going to be a pip. Maybe we'd better get humping on the maps after dinner unless you've got something better to do."

"Not a thing. That's a good idea. Thought maybe I'd go find my World War II base tomorrow. Be glad to have you for company."

"Sounds great. How far is it from here?" Harry always liked to explore new places. Being from Minnesota, I guess he didn't get to see many places.

"About a hour and a half. We take the Cambridge-Norwich train, and get off at Stowmarket, then get a cab to Rattlesden. Probably the base is a pasture now, but I'm sure we can find our way around."

"Jolly good show, sport. Let's give'er a go, as the Blokes would say." His attempt at English phraseology was far short of the mark, but it did sound like me 13 years ago.

"Righto, we'll hop off after an early breakfast. We can catch the 9:00 a.m. train."

Chapter 20

ENGLAND AND THE PAST

"Two tickets to Stowmarket, please," I asked the stationmaster, having to stoop down to see him in the railroad station ticket cage. "Are you sure you want off at Stowmarket, mate? There's nothing there, now."

"We're planning on going on to Rattlesden, then to the old air base. I was stationed there in 1943," I replied.

"Right you are. I remember it. My sister and her family live outside Rattleden. I remember you Yanks back then. You were a wild bunch, and that's a fact. You'll only find sheep and cows, now," he reminisced, handing us our tickets and change.

The train was right on time, and we climbed aboard a third class compartment. It was empty, and had the same musty smell most English trains do. As we settled ourselves near the windows, the train whistled, and, with a jerk, pulled away, gathering speed swiftly.

As the countryside flashed by, I tried to visualize the base outside the small village of Rattlesden, but it was hazy, in my mind, and the vision was indistinct. Regardless, I felt a certain tingling feeling, in anticipation of moving into memorable surroundings.

"Next stop Stowmarket," said the conductor, sticking his head through the sliding door, leading to the aisle. "Step lively, now. The engineer won't stop long. He wants to stay on schedule," he cautioned, shutting the door, and moving on.

After our fast exit, the train pulled out of the station, steam billowing from under the wheels. I walked to the stationmasters' office facing the railroad tracks, and noted that the train back to Cambridge wasn't until 3:00 p.m., giving us about four hours.

Harry had wandered around to the front of the station, found a taxicab and was explaining what we wanted. It's amazing, but no matter where you are in England, there always seems to be a taxi nearby. Rather refreshing, I thought. After a thorough explanation, the cab driver remembered where the base was, and agreed to take us there, wait for us and bring us back in time to catch the Cambridge train.

We passed through Stowmarket and headed into the countryside. After a few minutes we rumbled through the one street that made up Rattlesden, and I saw the local pub, the Golden Horse, where I had spent many hours, drinking that awful-tasting ale and eating boiled eggs, and playing darts with the locals. It was just the same, with the sign gently swaying in the breeze. Farther down the street was the same fish-and-chips shop. I was never able to figure out if the good taste of the fish was due to the newspapers they were wrapped in or not. In any event, it was always delicious.

As we finally reached the end of the old road, I could just make out the cement control tower, standing in the distance. It was about all that was left intact of the once-sprawling base. Several metal Nissin huts were clustered about in the distance. They were in various stages of decay. The cabbie pulled up at the wooden gate, overgrown with weeds, and, knowing "these Yanks" were crazy, shut off the car engine, and lit his pipe, if for no other reason that he had nothing better to do. The grass was waist high, and as we tromped towards the buildings, I remembered much the same scene depicted in a famous movie about the Eighth Air Force. The cows, scattered around, didn't even seem to be aware of our presence.

As we approached the tower, Harry said, "Bring back memories?" As we sat down with our backs against the concrete I scanned the area, the flat landscape, the hedges that surround any sizable plot of ground in England, the cows grazing on the lush greenery, my thoughts did, indeed, go back over the years. Many faces, those of my crew, of Tom, Ed, Sparky, Ray, Gus, Norm and the others, who shared the fun, horror, fright and satisfaction I experienced, flooded back to me as I sat in the warm English midlands sun. The crash landings, the fog nemesis on return from a long mission, the red flares indicating the wounded aboard a laboring B-17, the mutilated skin of the Flying Forts, all of these things came to me.

"You'll never know, Harry. Let's go get a drink in Rattlesden and I'll tell you about it. The tower, here, is the only thing I recognize, and I doubt if anything else is worth trying to find.

As we emerged from the overgrown field, the cab driver was taking a nap, oblivious to everything. When we opened the cab door, he opened his eyes, and cast a questioning look our way.

"How about stopping at the Golden Horse, and having a drink with us?"

"Righto, governor, I'm for that." We thundered off, as if the saloon would run dry before we got there. A few chickens, used to the serenity of their domain, will never be the same.

The town of Rattlesden was just the same. I suspect it hadn't changed in over a hundred years. Quaint, solid and nostalgic all fit any description of this place. It is hard to explain, but the small towns of England all seem to emit an air of age, and steeped in tradition. It's something not evident in any town in the United States. As we opened the bar door, the smell of pipe tobacco, beer and whiskey rushed to meet us. The place was dark, as are most English pubs, and the barkeeper scarcely looked up as we entered. It was empty of people, except for us.

Harry and I had scotch, and the cabbie a "mild and bitters." As we sat down at a well-worn table, Harry reminded me I had a story to tell. My tale has been told, in one fashion or another, in many war books. Suffice it to say, I told him of my being shot down near Paris, escaping from the Wehrmacht, getting with the French underground, bicycling through Belgium, Holland and Denmark, making my way across the Baltic on a fishing boat, finally getting to Malmo, Sweden, and being flown back to England in a RAF Mosquito; the epitaph was finishing my tour of combat, without further major mishap. Unless, of course, you don't count five crash landings as a result of battle damage. On the positive side, I finished my 30 missions, shot down two German fighters confirmed and rode the *Queen Mary* back to New York City.

* * * *

"Governor, we'd best be moving along, if you intend to make the Cambridge train," the cabbie suggested. Harry and I looked at each other, and broke out in a good laugh. It seemed almost sacrilegious to break my trend of thought, but the imperturbable Britisher was right. We paid up, got back into the cab, and got the train back to Upper Heyford.

The trip back went by quickly. My reverie had been broken, and there seemed no reason to dwell on it any longer. Harry, seeming to understand, said nothing. What is past is gone, and no need to try to recover it.

Chapter 21

TEXAS LEAGUE BRIEFING

"Gentlemen, this is the main briefing for Texas League. Classification is secret until 24 hours after the last aircraft lands at Lake Charles." It was 10:00 a.m., December 4, 1955.

"Takeoff for the first wave is 2000 (8:00 p.m.) December 5 (tomorrow)," 8:00 p.m. was local time, six hours later than at Lake Charles. "Each wave will consist of two flights of four B-47s each, 30 minutes spacing between waves. Tankers will be from the 44th and 68th Refueling Squadrons, in place at Harman and Goose. Offload will be 45,000 pounds. Flight time 11 hours and 30 minutes, Colonel?"

The Boss took the stand, glanced at the captive and uncommonly attentive audience, and started, "This is the big one. No flight plans will be filed, no interplane communications, radio silence rendezvous and refueling, no contact will be made until you have departed the target areas. Then, and only then, will you identify yourself. IFF will be placed in "standby" until you are over the target. You can expect fighter attacks, but if you don't try to cut corners, Air Defense forces will not be alerted until after you enter the U.S. SAC wants to put the pressure on them .

"Fuel will be critical if you don't get the scheduled onload. Weather in the refueling area is marginal, and the tanker bases are zero zero, now. If we can't get our tankers launched, the mission will be delayed. Final crew briefing will be at 1100 tomorrow. See you then. You are excused, unless there are any questions. The DO is available. Bernie?"

One AC, from the 68th, stood up, and posed the question on the minds of more than one of us. "Colonel, what happens if we can't get our fuel?" The DO, shuffling his feet, simply said," I don't know, but don't worry about that. I'm confident you can do the job." My sweet mother, I thought, what is that clown think he's doing. I couldn't believe my ears. Harry just shook his head, and Bob cursed under his breath.

There were no more questions. The crews didn't have much to say as they filed out. Harry, Bob and I completed our flight plans by using the latest winds supplied by the cooperative weather officer. I spent the next hour annotating all the bases within 100 miles of our course, with runways of 8,000 feet or more. This was in case we had an emergency or our fuel became critical and we weren't able to reach our destination. In as much as we had to fly formation to the refueling area, we would not plan for any celestial fixes, unless the radar went out. We could still use radio fixes, but they weren't accurate enough for precise navigation. Radar would continue to be our best bet.

Once through with our flight planning, the three of us went through the entire mission, hour by hour, action by action, so that we missed nothing that could help us. If I missed something, Bob invariably caught it. If Bob missed something, Harry always found it. Once we left the refueling area (over the Greenland ice cap), we were on our own. We wanted to be ready for the task ahead, and I felt we were. We put away our gear, and went down to the flightline, to check on the "Prowler."

"Enjoy London, Vince?" I asked, as we watched our crew chief checking the alternator on the No. 3 engine. It was housed in the nose cone.

"You really know how to hurt a guy, Sir. I could have stayed another week, if my money hadn't run out. Those dollies are really something else. How about you all?"

"Oh, we enjoyed Westminster Abbey and the change of the guard," Harry jokingly told him. "If it hadn't been for all those girls pestering the AC everywhere we went, we could have enjoyed ourselves," he added, knowing full well he didn't believe a word we said. Bob was glaringly quiet. As a matter of fact, he made a point of looking at the ground power unit. I would have to quiz him later.

"I checked her out this morning, Major. No. 3 alternator was acting up, but I found a loose lead and she's fixed now. Could you run up the radar, Captain? I wouldn't let these local clowns touch it. I'm not sure they know what's going on with a MA-7." Our particular radar set was new to SAC, and there weren't many technicians checked out on them, especially in the forward (overseas) areas.

The radar in 240 was a personal thing with Harry. He knew it inside out and really got upset if someone played around with it. Each crew normally got to fly "their" airplane, but not always. The more you use the equipment of one aircraft, the better it becomes, for each crew member can help the maintenance technicians to "peak" the aircraft and systems into achieving its best capabilities. Vince knew this and guarded against anyone who wanted to "check it out," unless he knew him. We had some excellent radar technicians back at Lake Charles, but only one of them came over to England with us, and he had a lot of trouble with other aircraft, and couldn't get to preflight ours in time. So, one of the base people was supposed to do the job, but our crew chief didn't know him, and wouldn't let him touch it. Harry was duly grateful.

"No sweat, Sergeant, I'd rather do it myself, anyway. Fire up the APU (ground power unit), and I'll give it a good check-out."

As Vince got the unit started, I told Harry that Bob and I would go over to Weather and would meet him there. He nodded as he climbed aboard.

Chapter 22

THE FRUSTRATIONS

The days from December 5-8 of 1955 were ones of frustration, caused by the abominable weather over Greenland, Iceland and northeastern Canada.

"Major, the weather stinks over all of Newfoundland. Those tankers don't stand a snowball's chance in hell of getting off, much less back in. You're not going anyplace tonight. See this cold front?" He pointed to an extensive frontal system on the weather map laid out in front of us. "It's a real deep one. Barometer's been falling all along the front, and this low, here, is deepening. The front won't clear out for at least three days, maybe four. Fog and snow all over the eastern seaboard. The refueling area should be OK, but the upper air charts show a lot of instability, so you could have a real problem between 14 and 22,000 feet, with contrails and a lot of turbulence. No, I'd say you'd have to wait for this one, like it or not. Your boss wasn't too happy about what I told him. Guess he thought I could do something about that damned stuff. As a matter of fact, a C-54 came in from Iceland about two hours ago, and he was just thankful he made it. Apparently he got one hell of a lot of ice at about 8,000. I talked to one of the passengers, and he told me several of them got sick on the flight." With that little bit of wisdom he gave me a hard stare, shook his head and went back to his charts.

Every time we fly, we have to get a weather briefing before we file our route clearance, but I've found that you get a better picture if you talk to the weather man before you plan your flight. You've got more time and can ask more questions than just before flight time. It's helped me many times before, and it's become a habit to do it this way. I guess I picked it up while I was flying on the Berlin Airlift in late 1948 and 1949. Too many times a pilot can get backed into a corner if he doesn't know all the factors that can affect his decisions.

"Dave, the DC's passed the word. The mission's delayed 24 hours. Next crew briefing is tomorrow at 1400," Harry said, as Bob and I were having a cup of coffee and a donut in the crew lounge at Base Ops.

"I'm not surprised, after what the weather man just told us. It looks like more than 24 hours to me. You two go have lunch. I'll tell the crew chief, in case he hasn't heard. Meet you at the mess."

* * * *

"Gentlemen, after three days of delays, SAC says we are going tonight. Goose and Harmon are above minimums, so Texas League will go. We received the SAC execution order about an hour ago. Unfortunately, the weather in the refueling area doesn't look good at all, but we're going, anyway. Any questions?"

"Colonel, what happens if we can't get our fuel?" asked one of the crew members.

"Just play it by ear, I guess." Now that was a real beauty of an answer, I thought, glancing at Bob. He was frowning, looking at the floor in front of him. The DO obviously hadn't considered that. It's awfully hard to decide where to go if you can't get you fuel, you're over northern Greenland, on a classified mission, and the weather stinks all over the place, and you could expect fog back at Upper Heyford. Yes, this was a real beautiful answer to give to a crew, especially from one who's supposed to know what he's doing. I secretly hoped he would get himself into that predicament, but he was riding in the fourth seat with one of the most experienced aircraft commander and best refueler in the business, and he knows it. He wasn't much of a pilot, and he knew we all knew it. Not the kind of a leader you could place your faith in.

I again glanced at Bob, and he just looked up at the ceiling. "Bernie's in good form today," Harry caustically muttered. Harry had a personal grudge with the DO. He blocked Harry from going to graduate school, even though I had recommended him. I would have hated to lose Harry, but his master degree was more important for his career. We had been named Wing crew of the month six times, crew of the quarter four times, and was nominated for SAC Crew of the Month honors four times, primarily because of our domination in bombing and navigation accuracy. It was understandable that the DO would be hesitant to lose such an outstanding observer, but it was pure selfishness that he barred Harry from advancing himself. As I pointed out during several discussions with the DO, aggressive and competent officers who could be advanced to staff positions should not be discouraged. Unfortunately, too many ranking officers in the lower echelons were only thinking of their own position, and not the welfare of the service, or of outstanding young officers. This is one of the reasons the caliber of the Officer Corps in the Air Force has not been as consistently high as it could have been.

The two days before the execution order were ones of frustration. The front had stalled and the weather stayed bad all over. We spread our time between re-planning, eating, sleeping, playing cards and visiting the Base Exchange. Nerves were getting frayed. Several times heated discussions occurred between normally-close friends. Everyone was on edge, from crew chiefs up to the old man. Rumors started flying that the mission would be canceled because of a probable decay in security. I'm sure SAC was hopping up and down, because it had a sizable force, ineffectively pinned down by conditions out of their hands. Finally, the word was flashed to us - GO. In retrospect, it was a poor decision, as the events will bear out. For us at the tail end of the string, it was to become a nightmare, and, as you will see, the almost ultimate test of the capability of man and machine to overcome an impossible situation, one beyond the control of many of us. Of course, hindsight is always better than foresight, but even now I seriously doubt if the decision was the right one.

The Wing CO, in a significant move, took over the final briefing. Word had gotten around that he was extremely unhappy with the way the DO had handled the previous briefings. He looked haggard from the obvious pressure, and his personal thoughts were revealed as he laboriously outlined what was in store for us. He didn't paint a pretty picture, but at least it seemed he was being honest with us.

"The 44th and 68th Wings will launch tonight, first aircraft takeoff at 2000 (8:00 p.m.). Refer to your flimsies for individual departure times. Refueling will be as briefed previously, onloads as indicated. Don't look for any extra fuel. There isn't any. There are no spare tankers, so you cannot look forward to additional support in case one of them aborts. If you don't have a tanker, don't horse around, come on back home. Takeoffs on schedule are critical. There will be no late takeoff, repeat, no late takeoff! Weather in the refueling area is marginal. Those aircraft unable to get their fuel will have to make their own decisions based on their circumstances. Weather says the weather may not hold here. Fuel will be critical upon arrival back here if the weather is bad; don't take any chances. If you can't get your fuel and have to return to the UK (United Kingdom), don't hesitate to break radio silence, but only under those conditions! Remember, and I can't stress this too strongly, once you descend to air refuel, you're committed to return to England, if you can't get fuel.

"You will note winds are higher than originally predicted." The Old Man was talking more rapidly, now. It had its effect on all of us. Some of the crew members were chain smoking, while others were fidgeting in their seats. The pressure was beginning to build.

"That is because of a strong jet stream moving in on our route. Flight times will have to be adjusted to make up lost time at control points, but don't cut any corners." His voice betrayed his feelings. He was now speaking louder. I looked around the room and my concern was reflected on the faces of many of the more experienced crew members. He continued.

"There are no alternates in Ireland, Iceland, Greenland, Newfoundland or Nova Scotia. You'll have to make your decision at the descent point to refueling. Once you descend, you're committed, one way or the other. One last thing in our favor: The refueling time has been extended 10 minutes to compensate for the bad weather. The tankers will give you as much fuel as they can, but each tanker has two receiver flights, so don't expect much more than your scheduled offload. Each control point will be extended 10 minutes, so make the adjustment. That's it, gentlemen. See you at Lake Charles. If it's any consolation, I told SAC the mission could go to hell, in a hurry. But we still go."

As the Wing CO left the podium and walked out of the briefing room, no one moved. It was hard to believe SAC was going to commit almost 80 aircraft and nearly 40 tankers to a condition with so many unpredictable variables in a peacetime situation. No one said anything, but it was easy to see what was going through the minds of these professional fliers. Most of them had never been placed in such a position as this.

Chapter 23

Texas League

It was December 8, 1955, and, as I sat in the relative quiet of the ejection seat of B-47 No. 240, with the noise of the ground power unit filtering through my crash helmet, I got mad all over again. I was fuming over the comment made by our gutless Director of Operations, when he left us out on a limb if we couldn't get our fuel. My thoughts went back to our arctic survival course. One particular instructor laid it right on the line to us. "If you have to bail out in the Arctic, your chances are slim to none for survival," A very comforting thought. At that time, the Air Force didn't have the worldwide search and rescue capability that was developed a few years later.

Crash landing at night really can be hazardous because of a lack of vision and perception, but to try to put the bird down on snow and ice can really be disastrous. Any white surface can present an illusion of height as you approach it. It would be very easy to drive the nose right into the snow, and that would most assuredly cause the plane to break up and probably one or more of the crew would be injured, or killed.

The alternative to crash landing in the Arctic, would be to eject, but, in doing so, the flier will lose the sanctuary of the airplane to protect him from the elements, plus loss of a lot of survival gear. To put it bluntly, our position was one of being between a rock and a hard place.

My thoughts went back to another one of SAC's survival courses, a mandatory requirement for all combat crew members. Usually two or three crews trek into the wilds with a professional guide to instruct them, and they are to "survive" for a specified number of days, using their ingenuity to stay alive. Unfortunately, the course in Alaska was different. The last three days were without a guide, but the crew had a portable radio to maintain contact with the home base. A series of events that followed this particular crew resulted in a disaster. Out of nowhere, on the second day of being on their own, a devastating storm struck. Rescue crews could not get to them, the atmospheric conditions rendered the radio inoperable, and the 60 mile-per-hour winds blew away the protective tents. Result: one crew member froze to death, one froze his feet, and one almost died from exposure. A nice thought to be carrying around when they were possibly about to be placed in a similar situation. It didn't help my confidence, waiting for the time to start engines.

* * * *

"Olive Flight, start engines." As the turbine wheel of number four engine started to turn, I could see the first flight taking off, lights blinking and the fiery exhausts leaving an illuminating trail into the black, foggy night.

"Olive Flight, starting to taxi." We moved out onto the taxiway, the "tail-end Charlie" of four B-47s. As we passed the last B-47 of the next flight, I noticed the AC waving, and then clasped his hands over his head, as if to say, "Good luck. You'll need it."

"Decision speed, now" Bob called, as the aircraft accelerated past our "go-no go" point. Our airspeed was right on the money, and we rocketed down the runway.

"Takeoff speed, now!" The end of the runway was dangerously close as I applied more back pressure to the monster. She staggered off under the heavy load, and I called for gear and flaps up, with my eyes riveted on the plane ahead of us. "No. 2 EGT is high. I'm reducing the throttle," Bob advised, as I felt No. 2 being reduced. "Gear is up, flaps are up."

"Outbound heading is 328. Radar is OK. I've got them. Your position is good, closing on number three." Harry's voice was crisp and reassuring. We went through a cloud deck at 6000 feet and got a little ice on the engine nose cones. I temporarily lost the aircraft ahead, but our radar had kept me closing on them. At

9000 we broke into the clear, and I saw the other three ahead and above, wing lights blinking.

No. 2 is breaking off to the right," Harry announced. I could see Jack Chartiers aircraft sliding away from the formation, and passed us about two miles to our right, obviously in trouble. As it turned out later, he had radar trouble and returned safely to Heyford before the weather closed in. How many more?

Once in loose formation to the right of the lead aircraft, I engaged the autopilot and took stock of our condition. I started fuel transfer, but did not transfer out of the two 10,000 pound (fuel capacity) wing tanks, because they take twice as long to fill as the internal tanks. I figured that saving time in refueling would help us. On the other hand, I always ran the risk of failure of the external tanks to transfer into the mains, with subsequent non-usable fuel (about two hours worth), but that was a calculated risk I was going to take, considering what was ahead.

The wing tanks on the B-47 were always a nemesis. They were designed to extend the range of the bird, and then be jettisoned when empty. This concept was to be used in wartime, but under peacetime conditions we used them all the time. These tanks had no booster pumps, rather relied solely on air pressure(from the engines) to force fuel into the main fuel tanks, and frequently one or both failed to function. The result was 10,000 or 20,000 pounds of unusual fuel. This "dead weight" caused a loss of more than two hours of airborne time, plus a possible overweight landing condition. If only one of the wing tanks malfunctioned, the problem was magnified because the B-47 pilot could only use about half of the one good tank's fuel, then he would not be able to maintain lateral control. To get rid of these tanks, the pilot electrically released the retaining pin, and that allowed the wing tank parachutes (mounted in the extreme rear of the tanks) to operate, pulling the tanks off the wing via rails. During operational tests, one of the wing tanks being jettisoned would "hang-up" and the pilot had to land with a small parachute streaming behind the wing, and the tank partially back on the rails. This was not a healthy situation, but one we had to face on every flight.

As we leveled off at 33,000 feet, everything was normal. The Prowler was handling beautifully, and there were minutes of silence, each of us with our own thoughts. Bob tuned in the Reykjavik (Iceland) beacon, and the homing needle registered the station ahead and to the left. I informed Harry, and he confirmed he had the south coast of Iceland on the extreme edge of his scope at maximum range.

"Aircraft, one o'clock above and coming this way." Bob was scanning the sky around us. I looked up from taking a fuel reading, and sure enough, there were lights flashing about 3,000 feet above us. It obviously was a B-47 from the speed, size and location.

"There's another one, Dave - twelve o'clock high. They must be running into trouble in the refueling area." This one came right over the top of us. Another B-47. It was impossible to tell if it was one of ours or from the 68th Wing. They had launched from RAF Fairford an hour before us, using our tankers first. The air refueling points for the two bomber wings were 60 miles apart and the return altitude and direction were nearly the same. As it turned out, they were 68th planes from earlier flight, unable to get their fuel. We were to find out why shortly.

Chapter 24

THE TERROR - NIGHT MASS AIR REFUELING

"Dave, I've got the tanker beacons ahead at 150 miles," Harry advised. "Start descent point in 80 miles. Can't tell how many tankers, their blips are merged at this distance."

By pre-arranged signal, the lead plane copilot flashed us a Morse code "S" (with his flashlight) one minute before starting descent to refueling, although this really wasn't necessary, for the handbook charts were specific on how far back the B-47 should start down, based on altitude difference of the KC-97 and the B-47. They were supposed to be at 17,000 feet and we were at 33,000. Descent range was 75 miles.

"Start descent in 10 seconds," Harry cautioned. "It looks like only three tankers; their orbit point is 20 miles too far west. The heading is 345 instead of 360." What's going to happen, now, I wondered. If Harry was correct and there were only three tankers, then we had a problem, for we had four bombers! Harry settled that, for he amended his earlier statement. "Dave, there's a fourth tanker off to the right, but his beacon is intermittent. Looks like he may be the spare." Anticipating the descent, I slowly moved the throttles back, pushed over and pegged the airspeed at 280 knots.

"The two others are still at 33,000, Dave. Something's wrong," Bob exclaimed. "We're right on, Dave," Harry insisted. Don't level off now. I've got our tanker isolated. Correct 5 degrees right. His beacon is still in and out, but I can hold him OK." Harry recognized something wasn't right, and didn't wait for me to tell him to take over. As it turned out, our decision to go alone was a good one, for the leader was having radar troubles, his beacon was intermittent, his radar operator was indecisive, and No. 2

kept waiting for the leader to start down. As a consequence, the two overshot by 10 miles, before No. 2 realized what had happened. He immediately started down, followed by the No. 1 aircraft, but they wasted valuable time that they couldn't recover from. Then the thought flashed through my mind. In my haste to figure out the refueling, I forgot one of our bombers had turned back, early, and we wouldn't, in fact, have too many bombers for tankers after all. I heaved a sigh of relief.

"The tankers have turned on course, and they're spread out. Turn seven degrees left at 40 miles." I was passing through 30,000 feet, intending to bottom out at 16,500 feet, 500 feet below the scheduled altitude of the tankers.

"Thirty miles, on course," Harry advised. "We're closing awfully fast. I hope their airspeed is up," he commented. Passing through 25,000, I had let my airspeed build up, now reading 315 knots.

"Bob, can you see the other two?" I asked, concerned as to where they were. Night refueling, in a group effort, has been described as the ultimate terror. This one was developing into a real wild one. "I lost them about two minutes ago, above and behind us. Looks like weather ahead," Bob warned.

"20 miles, closing fast. On course."

As I passed through 21,000, the aircraft shook and vibrated, the wings flapping wildly, much like we had passed behind another planes, propwash. We were in the clouds. I turned on the IFR lights. Ice was clearly visible on the engine cowlings.

"Ten miles, straight ahead. My radar elevation indicates we're through their altitude." My God, I thought, maybe we wouldn't have any more trouble.

"I'm in the clouds, Harry. I'll bottom out at 18,500, now, Bob, you've got the fuel panel. Keep your eyes open. They may be above the clouds."

"There they are, ahead and above us," Bob yelled. As we intermittently were in the clear. The aircraft was vibrating. I looked up and saw them, then lost them when the clouds closed in again.

We were picking up more ice on the nose and windshield, and the wings were really flapping from the unstable air. Things were falling apart fast.

"Five miles, two degrees left and above." That did it. I eased the nose up, added power and, at 20,000, we broke out. There they were three of them, two together and one spaced off to the right, still slightly above our altitude. We found out much later that the fourth tanker aborted just as we started our descent. He had engine problems, and went back into Goose Bay.

"Three miles ahead, slightly above." I was sure they weren't at their forecasted speed, so I slowed to 220 knots, knowing I'd lose 10 knots when we lowered 20% flaps, plus another 5 knots when the IFR door opened. Then the reason for the problem came to me. They obviously couldn't maintain formation at the scheduled altitude, so they were flying just above the cloud deck with no way to tell us. We never did find out why they were 20 miles off course, and the refueling heading was 15 degrees off.

"One mile, closing, good airspeed loss. We're in good shape." Gauging distance at night is tough, and I relied exclusively on Harry until we got within a half a mile. From then on, it's all up to me. I continued our gradual climb towards the tanker, adjusting the power to maintain a speed of 220 knots.

"One half mile, closing slowly. Looking good. I'll keep the radar "on" until we're in the observation position, just in case." I gave Harry the OK, and kept boring into the observation position.

We were buffeting from the condensation trails coming from the tanker engine exhaust gases, freezing the sub-freezing temperatures.

"Bob, open the door," I ordered, as we were sliding into the dead spot, behind the tanker. There's a vacuum about 100 feet behind and 25 feet below a KC-97 that is devoid of aerodynamic air. If you can find this spot, you can stabilize the power, trim, and then move into position. A fleeting thought. Hell, man, you're committed!

No turning back, now.

"Darn, he's got his boom stowed," I exclaimed, as I jockeyed the bird into position, desperately fanning the rudders and yo-yoing the throttles. This means he wasn't ready to refuel. (We found out later he was the spare, and would take over if one of the primary tankers didn't show up. He surely knew the No. 3 tanker had aborted, so he should have been ready to refuel in his place. Why he wasn't I never did find out). This made no sense, so I reached forward of the throttles and flashed the landing lights several times. The boomer must have been in the refueling pod, because the boom immediately came down into the trail position. We were losing valuable time and fuel. The radio silence restriction was really working against us. My left wing got into the tanker slipstream, we slued into a violent buffeting, and the ice started building up again from the ice crystals from the tanker exhausts. We began to shake, violently. I corrected by fighting the controls and the boomer moved the boom up and down, indicating he was ready to go. Thank God.

Night refueling, under the best of conditions, requires maximum concentration and physical dexterity, for you have no references to gauge you position and closure speed, except for the director lights. A radio silence hook-up is worse, for the boomer can't "talk you in," and when the tanker is fighting turbulence, the receiver has to fight it two-fold. This tanker AC was really having his problems as I slid into the "contact" position.

Wham! "Contact," Bob announced. "Fuel starting to flow." I was really on the end of a roller coaster. Suddenly, the tanker lurched, and I hit an upper limit disconnect. I added power to stay close.

"Disconnect," Bob called, and quickly punched the reset button, readying our system for another contact. "Ready for contact."

"Fuels gushing out of the boom. His poppet valve must be frozen open," I angrily cried. Fuel was flooding over our nose, the canopy, and the left side of the fuselage as the boomer moved the boom out of the way. In doing so he inadvertently sent a gusher of fuel into our left inboard engines. "Everyone go on 100% oxygen," I yelled over the intercom.

"Flameout on No. 3, "Bob yelled. I didn't have time to glance at the instruments. I put No. 3 throttle in cutoff, and quickly advanced the remaining five throttles to compensate for the loss of thrust. "Bob," I yelled, "Center the needle and ball with the trim." I didn't dare look at the instruments, or I would have lost the tanker, for sure. Things were really getting hairy. The acceleration moved us right back into the contact position, and the boomer wisely slammed the boom into the receptacle, thus stopping any more fuel from escaping. The whole plane shuddered from the impact.

"Damn," exclaimed Harry. "I thought the boom was coming right into my lap. Stay with him," he encouraged.

"Fuel's coming in. We've got 10,000 pounds. Hang on," Bob said." Don't let him get away. Your power is good and the trim is set." Those words were like music to my ears.

The temperature outside was a minus 50 degrees centigrade, but I was sweating all over, and my arms were beginning to feel the strain.

"Twenty thousand pounds. Disconnect. Ready for contact."

The tanker was having his problems, and I just couldn't counteract his wild antics fast enough. The sweat was pouring down my cheeks. Fortunately, when the boom disengaged, the poppet valve seated, so we didn't have that to worry about, again. I moved back in from an outer limit disconnect, and he socked it to me, again.

"Fuel coming. 25,000 pounds. Tanks filling evenly, even with No. 3 caged. Powers' approaching the critical point." We were power limited to 98% RPM, under sustained conditions. With only five engines I was having to use extra power to keep us in the refueling position. It was getting tight.

"End of A/R in 10 minutes," Harry advised. "You've been with him for 15 minutes." My back, arms and legs were aching from all the physical effort. Now that we were getting heavier, it seemed as though we weren't being thrown around so much. Thank God for small favors, I thought, as I manhandled the controls to stay with him. All of a sudden, the tankers left wing dropped violently and I was thrown to the right, but I slammed left rudder, nudged the ailerons, and stayed with him. God, I'm tired, I thought. I shrugged my shoulders several times to stave off the creeping stiffness.

"30,000 pounds and still coming. He'd better cut down the pressure before too long." Great. All I need is a pressure disconnect.

"35,000 pounds, looking good. Power is running out at 97%." The Prowler was responding more slowly due to the loss of an engine. The weight was overtaking the power available. "Should have enough to finish..." Bob didn't have time to complete his thought, for we slued to one side as the tanker went to the other, and we got a right limit disconnect. As Bob reset the system, I went back at the boom, working furiously with the controls and throttles. We slid back into position and the boom slammed home, once more.

"Contact, 38,000 pounds now. Another couple of minutes and we'll have it. Stay with him, buddy," Encouraged Bob. "Easy, we're running out of power."

"Five minutes to end refueling."

"Roger, Harry. Bob, can you see the others?"

"No, but about five minutes ago one of the 47s went underneath us. Looks like he couldn't get enough fuel. 41,000 pounds, just a little longer. Come on, Daddy."

The tanker AC was really fighting to maintain a stable platform, and I was lucky to stay with him. There was no more power available. In what seemed an eternity, Bob finally said the magic words, "43,000 pounds." We'd better get out of here before we lose what we've got. You've been at maximum power for the past two minutes. Let's not push our luck." I knew I couldn't handle another disconnect, and I had been riding at the outer limit of the boom extension.

The boomer rattled the boom in the receptacle, and we both disconnected at the same time, he stowing his boom, and I just let the B-47 slide back and down for 30 seconds, raised the flaps and closed the IFR door, raised the nose and accelerated slowly to climb speed. The tanker slid from my vision, off to the left. It was over. The pit of my stomach was churning, almost uncontrollably. "Bob, can you see any of the others," I croaked, my throat so dry I could barely make a coherent sound.

"No, but the two other tankers are in the clouds. You're cleared to the left."

"Initial heading 225 degrees. I'm bringing up the radar, and will refine that when I get a radar fix."

The acceleration was slow, because of the dead engine and high gross weight. My mind started to work again. I was thinking of what had caused the engine failure. The Prowler was doing her best, but we were very heavy and the power just wasn't there. I was going to have to do something or we'd never make it back to Lake Charles. Finally, I made a decision. Once established on heading, I told Bob I was going to try to start No. 3, believing the flameout was due to fuel flooding and not an internal failure. The windmilling turbine should have cleared out the fuel from the tanker.

"It's worth a try. Standing by on No. 3, generator reset, voltage 28 and steady. Nothing wrong with the electrical circuit. I'm ready when you are." I turned on the air start switch, moved the throttle out of the cutoff position, noting the RPM was already 14%, due to the windmilling of the engine.

"Fuel pressure and oil pressure coming up. EGT rising," Bob called as I checked the engine exhaust gas temperature. If it rose past 700 degrees centigrade, I'd have to cut it off. The engine temperature rose fast to 650 degrees, then decreased to a steady 400. As I advanced the power on No. 3 to the same setting as the other 5, the engine stabilized and we were back in business. Another break in our favor. Would it last?

"Thank God you were right, Dave. We'd never have a chance on 5, Bob sighed.

My answer tumbled out in short, clipped spurts. "It had to be that way, Bob. There was no other possibility. It couldn't have been anything else, under the conditions we had." Vince, with a thumbs-up signal, handed me a hot cup of coffee.

I adjusted the trim, started fuel transfer out of the wing tanks, and they started pumping into the main tanks. That was a relief. Score another one for us. The coffee was delicious.

Chapter 25

Texas League Strike

"AC, this is radar. Set's on and in good shape. We're 50 miles north of course. I'm getting a radar wind. Stand by for a course correction." Harry was at it, again.

"AC, I've just checked our fuel, and we're 2,000 pounds below the line. We took too long getting the fuel, but we're still in good shape." I copied the fuel readings for my log, which would give Bob time to devote to celestial, if needed, and gunnery work.

Then Harry gave us the bad news. "AC, we're 10 minutes behind schedule. Wind is 280 degrees at 150 knots. That's 50 knots higher than forecast." Obviously, the jet stream had slipped further south than predicted.

Our crew had been together for two years, and we fed each other information as fast as we got it, so we all would be up to speed. I kept my own log, as did Bob and Harry. That way we could cross-check on each other. Harry kept the official log and map. We'd cross-check our positions whenever we got a fix, whether it be radar, celestial, or in my case, by multiple radio bearings and visual sightings.

"Leaving west coast of Greenland, 40 miles north of course. Prince Charles Island in 60 minutes, with the present ground speed. It's now 370 knots. Change heading to 230." Harry wasn't waiting for the stronger winds to blow us farther off course. Now that things had settled down, I tried to review what had happened.

We were darned lucky. Harry and Bob had done their job, but I wasn't satisfied I had done everything I could. It wasn't the best job I'd done, but we did get our scheduled fuel. We burned too much of it staying with the tanker and operating on five engines consumed a lot more. I was exhausted. As if he read my thoughts,

Vince, silent until now, handed me another steaming cup of coffee, smiling as he passed it to my waiting hand. It was pure ambrosia, and gradually I relaxed. We had been airborne more than five hours, and had about seven to go. Our target, the O'Hare Airport Tower at Chicago, was still four hours away. When you're busy the time flies, but when there's a lull, the physical fatigue overtakes you. The coffee helps and even the box lunch was something to look forward to.

"Leveling off at 35,000. My indicated is 252 knots. How does that check with your true airspeed, Harry?"

"Reading 430. That checks. Hold what you've got." We fly true airspeed on our missions. It's a complicated mathematical process to compute true airspeed (TAS). You have to figure altitude, outside air temperature and compressibility factor (wind pressure in the airspeed pitot tube on the side of the aircraft) on the computer. The temperature outside the plane must be monitored, for a five degree change in temperature will cause a large change in actual speed. It is much more accurate than flying indicated airspeed, because of the many variables. Fuel consumption is based on true airspeed and time. I adjusted the power to maintain the proper speed. We had used a lot of time getting to altitude, with high power setting, and that meant our fuel consumption would be more than we accounted for.

"Vince, put the steaks on the amplifier, please. All of a sudden, I'm hungry."

"I'm not surprised. You scared hell out of me. They've been there for 30 minutes, boss. Ought to be ready in another 15 minutes." There's a crew chief for you. God bless him, I thought. I leaned over and gave him a well-deserved "thumbs up."

One of the flight lunches available is cube steak, crackers, canned peaches, twinkies (my all time favorites), (raisins, milk and potato chips. The steak is wrapped in tin foil after it has been cooked at the flight kitchen, frozen and kept in the freezer until it is picked up by the flight crew. Once aboard, the steaks are placed on one of the racks of the radar set amplifiers, that heat up to over 100 degrees, and provide a good warmer for steaks and such. The only problem is you have to leave them there for 45 minutes, but they really taste good on a long mission. Some crews order two of these. The ingenuity of the crews again comes to the fore.

"Harry, I've got a two-station fix from Frobisher and Churchill, but it's not too reliable. For what it's worth, it puts us 30 miles from Prince Charles, 10 miles east of course. How does that check?"

"Looks good. I've got the crosshairs on the turning point. Center the PDI and we'll be in good shape. We're 15 minutes behind the control point time, but there isn't much we can do to make up that much time." Harry realized the situation, and knew that making up 15 minutes in one hour is impossible, so he didn't worry about it.

As I turned towards the turning point, both wing tank lights blinked, and then stayed illuminated, indicating they were empty. I waited a few minutes to see if the main tanks started going down, a double check that the wing tanks were, in fact, empty. They were, and I started transfer from the bomb bay tank. I had to reduce power, again, for we were getting lighter and it took less power to maintain the same speed. I would be doing this again and again. Less power meant less fuel consumption.

"Crew, this is AC. Starting climb to 37,000. "Our block altitude was between 33,000 and 39,000 feet, which means we could operate anywhere between those altitudes. FAA (Federal Aviation Agency, who controlled all traffic) was not aware of us, but we were the only ones in 1955 that could fly that high. As our weight reduced due to fuel consumption, we step-climbed. The higher you fly any jet the less fuel is used, and that extends the range. Texas League was really pushing the capability of the crews, and we took every advantage to save fuel. It paid off, time after time.

"Contrails are getting stronger," Bob advised. At our altitude, we were above the clouds, and the full moon made it look almost like daylight. Below us was a solid cloud layer, obscuring the ground.

"Dave, turn to 195. Coates Island in one hour. Wind has changed from 280 to 245 degrees, speed now 110 knots." Although the wind speed had reduced, the direction swung more on our nose, so we weren't getting much help, and we needed every break we could get.

"Ground speed is now 365. We're running 20 minutes behind the flight plan," Harry advised, confirming my thoughts.

"Fuel curve shows 4,000 pounds below the line. It's too early to tell, but we may be in trouble getting into Lake Charles," Bob added to Harry's appraisal. Things were going to hell in a hurry, I thought. Thinking ahead, I started considering alternate landing bases. Barksdale, 100 miles north of Lake Charles and a SAC base, was supposed to be good; Little Rock, 70 miles north of Barksdale was marginal, but we'd see as we passed right by it. Both were within visual range of our course, and I'd be able to see the weather far enough ahead to be able to decide by the time we got that far, unless something else went wrong. I wanted to get home after this fiasco, but we'd have to sweat it out.

The autopilot was holding the Prowler steady, fuel was transferring, and everything was under control. Harry had come back in the crawl-way to relieve himself. As he looked up, the moon illuminated his face. He was smiling, patted me on the knee, and got himself a cup of coffee. "You sure held on to that tanker. Just beautiful, Dave." He had been in "the hole," as we called the nose compartment, for over seven hours, and took the opportunity to stretch his legs, and relax for a few minutes. I patted his head as he went back forward. He was one in a million, and I felt a personal kinship with him that would last a long time.

Suddenly the airplane shook, the wings buffeting with reckless abandon. The turbulence cleared any cobwebs that may have been creeping over my mind. I noted the outside temperature had dropped three degrees. Oh! Oh! I thought. Another jet stream. There were no clouds at our altitude.

"Back on interphone. What's going on? Harry asked.

"The temperature's dropped. Better get a radar wind. Feels like a jet stream."

Two minutes later Harry advised the wind had shifted and picked up speed. Darn it, I thought. What else could go wrong? The buffeting continued.

"We're approaching Coates, 10 miles left of course. Turn right to 187 degrees. Lake Nipigon in two hours and 10 minutes. Ground speed now 350 knots."

"Aircraft at three o'clock, low." Bob's voice startled me, and I involuntarily jumped, grabbing the control column. I looked off the right wing, and saw indistinct lights. Obviously an aircraft, angling away from us. After two minutes, I lost sight of it. Wonder where he came from?

"Couldn't be one of ours. He's too far to the west. Must be a fighter," Bob commented. I looked at my map. The nearest Royal Canadian Air Force Base was about two hundred miles west of us.

"Dave, this sounds wild, but I've got an aircraft on my set, below and ahead. Crossing right to left," Harry blurted. "Can you see him, Bob?"

"Not yet. Where is he now, Harry?"

"About five miles at eight o'clock. He's turning left, and going towards six o'clock,"

"There he is! He's climbing at about seven o'clock, going away. Must be a RCAF CF-101. They're the only ones this far north. He's coming on my gunnery radar, now."

I swiveled my head around, and caught a glimpse of him, now almost behind and still below our altitude. "Keep tracking him, Bob. I doubt that he can catch us at this altitude and speed."

"Dave, turn further right to 192. That wind is a beauty." The constant turbulence was getting stronger, and the temperature had dropped another two degrees.

"He's still out there, AC. At three miles and still below." Bob had him locked on his radar.

Ten minutes later, he was five miles back and at our altitude. "It's a tail chase, but he's not gaining any ground. He must really be pushing to stay in range. He's breaking it off, now. He sure as hell must be low on fuel. I've got to give him an "A" for effort. He's off my scope, at seven o'clock and descending."

Our experience has shown us that if ground radar cannot get a fighter scrambled in time and get him up to us, the present fighter series can't catch us. This is why our route was as circuitous, to keep us away from Early Warning radar coverage. Fortunately for us, the fighters' range is limited, and if he can't get us early, he doesn't have enough fuel to prolong a chase.

"Somebody must have goofed on their flight plan and have alerted them," I guessed. "We're not supposed to get intercepted this far out. Keep on your toes, Bob." I made a note of the time and point of intercept on my map.

Chapter 26

BOMBING OF CHICAGO

We had been airborne eight hours, and were now approaching the United States/Canada border. We were about to make our run-in on Chicago, and I fleetingly thought that none of the citizens of Chicago would realize that on December 9, 1955, they would be "bombed" by the Strategic Air Command. The flight had been relatively quiet since that one fighter was after us, but then we hadn't expected that one. The buffeting had disappeared about an hour ago. It was smooth flying, now.

"Turn point in 50 miles. Center the PDI. IP in 20 minutes."

"Roger, Harry. I'll give you the bombing checklist. We'll let Bob stay with the gunnery radar."

As we turned towards the Initial Point (last prominent check point before reaching the target), I went through the checklist with Harry. We cross-checked altitude, airspeed, offset aiming point coordinates and a whole lot more. Our radar checked out perfectly.

"Over the IP. Turn left to 178 degrees. On the bomb run." I repeated the heading and changed to the proper heading. The autopilot was doing the work and operating well. "Three minutes to go," I advised.

"Roger. Crosshairs on the target. Give me control." I switched the autopilot to "remote," and now Harry was flying the aircraft with his radar controls.

"Your aircraft. Two minutes to go."

"Roger, I've got it. Looking good. Aiming point indistinct. Going to offset No. 1. Checks good. Going to offset No. 2. Beautiful. Going back to the aiming point."

"90 seconds to go," I interrupted.

"Roger. Aiming point not breaking up. Going to offset No. 2. Good. Will stay with it." He was locked on to Chicago-O'Hare airport control tower.

"Roger. 60 seconds. Check radar camera 'on.'"

"Roger. Checked 'on.' Offset No. 2 is good. Bomb release switches 'on.'"

"Bombing checklist completed. 30 seconds to go."

"Roger. We're in good shape. Standby for 'bombs away.'" The red "bombs away" light on my panel illuminated shortly thereafter. The bomb had theoretically been released.

"Bombs away. Hold heading for 30 seconds, then turn right to 190." I confirmed bomb release, and went through the post release check with Harry. "Completed. Right on target. That's a good run. OK to turn. Radar camera off.'"

Steady on the new heading, I was about to break radio silence and make my first radio call since leaving England.

"Chicago Center, this is Texas League Spiral Olive 4, over."

The answer was immediate. "Roger, Texas League Spiral Olive 4, this is Chicago Center. Go ahead."

"Chicago Center, Olive 4 here. Chicago at 20, flight level 370. I have a clearance for you. Are you ready to copy, over?"

"Go ahead, Olive 4. We don't have you in radar contact." I switched on the IFF.

"Roger, Chicago, Olive 4 requesting clearance from present position to Lake Charles Air Force Base, flight level 390. Direct St. Louis, direct Little Rock, direct. Time en route 2+05. Alternate will be Barksdale. 3+00 hours fuel. Over."

"Roger, Olive 4, copied. Have your squak now. What is your point of departure?"

They're going to love this, I thought. "Departure point classified, over."

"Understood, Olive 4. Squak 2, normal. Cleared as requested."

* * * *

I doubted if any Texas League aircraft had preceded us for Chicago Center sure didn't seem aware of the mission. That was a weird turn of events. As the lights of Chicago passed behind us, we could see St. Louis in the far distance, just a large smudge of light in the black void ahead on the horizon. I switched to the common weather frequency.

"Chicago weather, this is Olive 4. Over." I was concerned with the weather at Lake Charles for our last fuel reading showed us with only 9,000 pounds over the base, barring any more problems. We were 40 minutes behind flight schedule, and, as I climbed to 39,000 feet, it looked as though we were in trouble, if the weather worsened. Upper Heyford weather forecaster gave us 1,000 feet broken and three miles, in fog. A front had moved through Lake Charles last night, so fog could be expected as close as the base is to the Gulf coast. I asked Chicago weather for the present Lake Charles weather and what they would have for the next three hours. Also, I requested the Barksdale weather, our alternate.

"Roger, Olive 4. Lake Charles weather 800 feet overcast, 3 miles in fog. Temperature 50, dewpoint 49. Barksdale is below minimums, now 100 feet one half mile, fog; temperature/dewpoint 55/54; Little Rock, for your information, is 200 feet, 1/2 mile, drizzle and fog, temperature 54/53. No change forecasted for the next 2 hours, then lowering to minimums. Your request for Barksdale as an alternate should be reconsidered. Can you make it to Houston with your fuel on board?"

"Roger, weather. What is Houston/Ellington weather?" I asked. In as much as Houston was behind the front and only 15 minutes away from Lake Charles, at our altitude we could stretch it, but the Ellington runways were only 7,000 feet long. Something to consider.

"Roger, Olive 4. Ellington is 500 feet scattered, 2,000 feet overcast, 4 miles in fog. It looks like it will hold. What are your intentions, over?"

"OK, Chicago. We'll use Ellington as an alternate, instead of Barksdale. Will you pass to Chicago Center?"

"Roger, will do, Olive 4. Request your location and flight conditions?"

Harry provided the necessary wind conditions. "Dave, present wind over Chicago is 260 at 80."

"Chicago, present position 20 miles south of Chicago, at flight altitude 390; outside air temp is a minus 47; clear, wind 260 at 80; persistent contrails."

"Roger, Olive 4. Copied. Thanks for the info. Good trip."

It looked like the weather at Lake Charles could go down at any minute. From past experience we knew that if the surface wind was nil and a lot of humidity present, all it would take was three or four aircraft landing to stir it up and the fog would close the field. It had happened before. Not satisfied with the information I had, I decided to call the Whiteman AFB, Missouri, Command Post, have them patch me into the Lake Charles Command Post, through the SAC communications net. I thumbed through our comm flimsy, and found the code name for Whitman: Sinker. We were about a hundred miles from them but should easily be in contact with them at this altitude. Bob switched to the UHF (Ultra High Frequency) common SAC Command Post frequency,

"Sinker Control, this is Texas League Spiral Olive 4, over." No answer. I called again, this time with success.

"Roger, Olive 4. Go ahead. "

"Sinker, this is Olive 4. Patch me into Spiral Control, over." This was not a normal procedure, but our Operations Nickname gave us priority to use it."

"Roger, understand. Standby." They had to call SAC, who called the 44th, and then completed the circuit.

A few seconds passed. "Go ahead, Olive 4. Spiral is on the line."

"Spiral Control, this is Texas League Spiral Olive 4, estimating home plate at 0915Z (Greenwich time, or 0315 local Lake Charles time). How's the weather? Am short on fuel and understand weather will be marginal on our arrival, in two hours."

The voice that answered sounded excited. "Olive 4, weather presently 500 feet, 2 miles in fog. No wind, temperature/dewpoint 50/49. No, repeat, no Texas League aircraft have landed. Olive 2 just landed at Barksdale. No flight plans on anyone. What is your predicted fuel over base?" My God, I thought. Tex must really have been pushing it, to land at Barksdale when it was below minimums. Then I remembered he had our "play it by ear" DO slumbering in the 4th mans position.

"Roger, Spiral. Fuel on descent 9,000 pounds. Will check with you at 0830 Zulu, over Little Rock. Thank you. Out."

"Looks marginal, AC. Why not climb to 43,000 feet. That'll give us another 2,000 pounds," Bob suggested. He obviously had been hard at work with his fuel computer.

"Sounds good. See if you can get Kansas City for a clearance. We're in their control zone, now." Bob got us a clearance, and we swiftly climbed to 43,000 feet. Bob had turned around, and was now recomputing our fuel, for the umpteenth time, I bet. Bless him.

"The climb took us an extra 500 pounds, but we should save 2000."

What Bob was saying was we spent 500 pounds of fuel to climb from 39,000 to 43,000 feet, but in using less power to maintain the same speed at a higher altitude would reduce our fuel by 2,000 pounds in the two hours it would take us to get to Lake Charles.

"AC, this is radar. We're over St. Louis. We've lost another 3 minutes, but the wind speed is down to 75 knots," Harry said, encouragingly. Now all we have to do is sweat it out. It was very quiet in the Prowler. Vince was taking another nap, Bob was checking the fuel again, Harry was working his radar, and I was watching the instruments and recomputing our fuel at our higher altitude.

"Little Rock under the cross hairs. 50 minutes to Lake Charles," Harry advised, as the VOR radio station passed under us, as evidenced by the homing needle swinging around to our tail. The VOR was north of the city, so we had two minutes before turning on the last leg. I looked out and saw Shreveport ahead and to the right. The city's lights were showing through the overcast dimly. Bad news, I thought. As I turned onto our new heading, Bob was calling our Command Post.

Chapter 27

THE FINAL DECISION

"Olive 4, this is Spiral Control. Weather is 500 feet overcast, 1-1/2 miles in fog; temperature/dewpoint 50/50. Wind calm. Weather says you've got another hour at most. How's your fuel?"

"Roger, Spiral. Olive 4 here. We're down to 12,500 pounds at 43,000 feet. How's Barksdale?"

"Olive 4, Barksdale is below minimums now. What is your location and what are your intentions?"

I don't know why that question always bugged me, but it did. There they were, warm and cozy, without a care in the world, so to speak, and expected us to digest the information they just gave us and automatically spit out a response. Well, they would just have to wait a while. " Bob, tell them to stand by," which he did, knowing what was going through my mind. We had discussed this many times before and Bob knew my feelings about the subject.

The time for a decision was at hand and I was about to make it. "Bob, it looks like we can get in if we're lucky. I compute 6,000 pounds at touchdown, if we land out of a straight-in approach. Barksdale is no good and Ellington is still a possibility, if we don't horse around at Lake Charles. Let's give it a try. What do you think?"

"I agree, but I show a bit more than 6,000 pounds on landing. We've got enough for a second approach, but just barely."

"OK, tell them we're coming in." The biggest problem, at this point, was that a jet doesn't just burn fuel at low altitude, it literally gulps it down. Roughly, it took 4,500 pounds for a go-around, re-enter the traffic pattern, and get it on the ground. Using radar because of the bad weather took a lot more that I cared to think about. Bob advised Control of our decision and switched to approach control frequency. He would handle the radio communications from here on.

"Lake Charles approach, this is Texas League Spiral Olive 4, 120 miles north at flight level 430. Request straight-in approach. I want to descend straight in from 90 miles out with a GCA approach and landing."

Roger, Olive 4. Squak ident.... Roger, we have you at 110 miles. Maintain heading, and standby for straight-in approach from flight level 430, landing on runway 15. Present weather 500 feet and one mile, in fog, wind calm, altimeter 30-01. Call when ready to depart your altitude."

"Bob, we'll leave the gear up until we reach 20,000 feet. That should save us about 500 pounds. With the gear up, we could bring the power back to 40%, and let the airspeed build up without using extra fuel.

"Olive 4, 90 miles out. Start descent and turn right to 160. Call through 350 (35,000 feet) and 280 (28,000 feet)." Bob acknowledged.

"OK, sports, here we go." I brought the power back to 40% and lowered the nose. Bob called out the airspeeds.

"260, ... 270, ... 280, ... 290, ... 300, ... 310." I raised the nose slightly to maintain 310 knots indicated airspeed.

"Control, Olive 4, through 350." Harry kept us advised of where we were. "50 miles, Dave. Cross hairs on the runway." We were going down at 4,000 feet per minute. "40 miles out."

"Control, Olive 4 through 250." We were in good shape. Just about the right distance, maybe a little high. The increased pressure from the denser altitude was plugging up my ears.

"Olive 4, we have you 30 miles out, should be passing flight level 200." We were through 21,000. "Olive 4, continue descent to 4,000."

"Bob, drop the drag gear." When the drag gear came down the noise was abruptly deafening, and there was a lot of buffeting of the airframe.

"20 miles, Dave. PDI is on the runway." We were through 15,000 feet, still in the clear, but now our rate of descent increased to 6,000 feet per minute. The runway was five degrees right according to Harry's radar, but our heading would bring us in to the centerline. The pressure had build up in my ears faster, and I had a lot of trouble clearing them.

"Olive 4, what is your altitude?"

"Passing 8,000." My ears were aching, but I tried to ignore the pain.

"Roger. Continue descent to 2,000, complete landing check. Weather is now 400 feet and 3/4 mile. Call reaching 2,000. Your present heading is good." I was swallowing frequently to clear my ears. It didn't help much.

"12 miles out, Dave. They'll be turning you any time now," Harry interjected as we passed through 4,000 feet. I held the nose down, airspeed was 315 knots. Too fast.

"Approach, Olive 4 at 2,000 feet, heading 160." I unhooked my oxygen mask and blew my nose hard. My ears popped and the pain decreased, but was still a nagging ache.

"Roger, Olive 4. Turn right to 130, slow to approach speed. Pulling up the nose, we slowed rapidly, but it seemed like it took forever for the speed to dissipate. Finally we had slowed to 190 knots. I called for gear and flaps. All gear indicated "down and locked," and the flaps were set by Bob. I furiously adjusted the trim and nudged the power up, anticipating reaching approach speed.

"Gross weight 92,000 pounds, fuel 7,500, approach speed 110 knots," Bob called out. I repeated his figures and concentrated on stabilizing the aircraft as it continued to slow down. My ears had almost cleared, the pressure diminished. The pain had subsided, but my sinuses were acting up. I probably would have one hell of a headache after we got on the ground.

Chapter 28

LAKE CHARLES - THE LANDING

I was holding 2,000 feet and trimming the aircraft as the speed continued to decrease.

"Olive 4, approaching glide path, slow to approach speed." I felt like telling him I had everything out I could. She was slowing, 130...125...120.

"Olive 4, start descent. Turn right to 132, 20 feet high, on centerline. 10 feet high, 5 feet high, on glide slope. Nice correction. Resume normal rate of descent." We were in the weather, like a white sheet had been thrown over us, but no turbulence. At this weight, the bird was very sensitive on the controls.

"Turn left two degrees, 10 feet high. Bring her down." I lowered the nose slightly and left the trim alone, sliding to the left. The altimeter now was passing through 1,000 feet, and we were in the weather, solid. The airspeed was still a bit high and that accounted for me being high on the glide path.

"Three miles from touchdown on centerline, still 10 feet high. "The power was still back, and we were just about to approach final speed. Then the airspeed pegged at 110 knots. The bird was like a feather in the breeze at this speed and weight as I adjusted the power to hold the speed where it was. I had to be careful on round-out not to "balloon" back into the air.

"Two miles, 10 feet high and holding. Bring it down. Turn one degree right." The bird was stabilized and I was flying by trim and power, just lightly touching the controls. My ears began to pop.

"One mile, on glide path, on centerline. "Through 600 feet, airspeed good, rate of descent 500 feet per minute. Good.

"Bob, standby the chute," I said, as I noted two red warning lights flickering on the fuel panel out of the corner of my eye.

Due to the nosedown attitude of the B-47, the fuel was thrust forward, and there wasn't enough to cover the boost pumps in the aft main tank, hence the lights, but I didn't have time to worry about it. All six engines were running off of the common fuel manifold and that's all I needed to know. We were looking good, at this point.

"One-half mile, on glide path, on centerline. Do you have the runway in sight?" The ground radar controller was required to ask this question as an aircraft approached the field minimums.

"Not yet. Continue the approach," I yelled.

"Approaching minimum, one-fourth mile. If you don't have the runway in sight, pull up on heading 150, climb to and maintain 2,000 feet, and contact approach control" This was also a required call.

About halfway through the last controller's transmission, I saw the runway lights, turned on the landing lights, and wrestled the bird to the runway. We floated a long way before the wheels touched.

"Chute," I called, and almost immediately felt the chute deploy and we started to slow. The tail started to raise because of the light weight, and I gently, but firmly, pulled the control column back in my stomach, and felt the wheels grip the runway. I applied brakes, and, at the same time, made sure the power was in the idle position. If the friction brake on the throttle quadrant is not tight enough, the vibration of the aircraft will cause the throttles to "creep" forward. The windshield clouded over with the mist, so I braked harder and looked out the left side of the canopy to keep us aligned with the center of the runway. I couldn't afford to take the time to turn on the windshield wipers.

"2,000 feet left," Bob warned, so I cut 1, 2, 5 and 6 engines and we slowed noticeably. I used all the runway to slow down to taxi speed, turning off at the last runway cross taxiway, still going about 50 knots. As we turned the speed slacked off and we stopped at the intersection of the end of the runway and the last taxiway.

"Darn, I thought we were going off the end," Harry exclaimed. I didn't answer immediately. I suddenly was exhausted and realized I was drenched in sweat. We made it," That was a hairy one!

"Dave, I never thought you'd make it," Bob said, breathing hard.

Finally I swallowed and said, "That weather almost beat us. This monster just didn't want to stop, even after you pulled the chute. Let's get the hell out of here," and I jammed the two remaining throttles up to about 80% and the beast shot forward. We dropped the chute, Harry shut down his radar, and Bob called ground control. The "follow-me" jeep had to pull off the taxiway to avoid us hitting him. A stupid maneuver on my part, but I was exhausted and wanted to get our feet on the ground. The jeep turned around, raced ahead of us and made us slow down to a normal taxi speed. I'll bet he was wondering what maniac was at the controls of the B-47, and just what I thought I was doing.

"5000 pounds on the gauges, Dad. We cut this one awful close. Thank God its over," Bob sighed, his breathing sounding labored. When the fuel gages on the B-47 got below 2,000 pounds in the tanks, they were highly inaccurate. As it so happened, the forward main had 2,000 pounds, the center main 1,000 pounds and the aft main 2,000 pounds. That, indeed, was cutting it awful close. Had we had to go around and make another approach, we could easily have had two or more engines flameout because of fuel starvation and a nose-high attitude the B-47 encountered during a climb.

Harry broke my train of thought. "Flight time 12 hours and 15 minutes. I'm so tired I could sleep for a week," he knowing full well we had another two hours to go before we could crawl into bed. Maintenance debriefing, filling out forms, and a verbal report to the Wing staff duty officer. What a thrilling thought.

Chapter 29

TEXAS LEAGUE IS OVER

As we turned off the taxiway and entered the parking ramp, I was startled because there was one B-47 in our parking area and none in the 68ths. My God, I thought. What happened to the rest of them?

"Bob, can you see any '47s in the 68th area? There's one in our area and it wasn't on Texas League."

"Not a one. Man, it's scary. What happened to them?" The whole parking ramp was empty. It normally could hold over 50 aircraft.

"I don't know, but we're about to find out. There's two staff cars waiting for us." As we were motioned into our parking spot by a ground crewman brandishing flashlights. I opened the canopy and the rush of cold air never felt so good. It was like a shot in the arm. I breathed deeply and was immediately exhilarated. I felt better, and, as I locked the brakes and shut down No. 3 and 4 engines, I felt like a new man, even though I knew this feeling wouldn't last. It never did, although I had the same feeling many times before.

As I was unbuckling my seat harness and parachute straps, a hand slapped my leg. I looked down, and there was the Vice Wing Commander, Col. Cliff Pyle, who had stayed "at home" to "look after the shop," so to speak. He groped in the dark for my hand and shook it vigorously, and exclaimed, "Dave, we thought you wouldn't make it. How the hell did you do it?" he blurted. "You're the only one back. Nobody else got through."

The shock of his statement was unbelievable. I thought, 78 launched and only one back! What the hell happened?

Reading my thoughts and before I could answer, the Colonel said, "Never mind for now. Get your gear, put it in my staff car and we'll go to the Command Post. I want to hear about this one.

SAC has been burning up the wires." Something was weird about his attitude. The Vice Wing Commander was noted for his unemotional, placid approach to everything. He always was in the background and rarely said anything. He flew with us once and didn't say a thing during the entire eight hour flight. He did say "thank you," as he climbed into his waiting staff car after the end of the flight and sped off. Now he was like a kid at Christmas, waiting for the packages to be opened. Strange.

As we shuffled into the Command Post, it was immediately apparent that something wasn't right. Usually only the two duty controllers are working the console, but now I noted a Wing Staff Navigator talking on one of the phones, a Wing Operations Officer working with a clipboard full of paperwork, as well as the noncomms always there. In addition, the Command Post conference room, almost always vacant at this time of the morning, was alight, with an airman posting a map that covered the Texas League routes of the 44th Wing aircraft. To one who has never been in a SAC Command Post, the immediate impression is one of noise, confusion, an impressive array of communications, and, in my mind, the peculiar odor of electronic machinery. Each bomb wing has direct communications with the USAF Command Post, SAC, each numbered Air Force, and units under the jurisdiction of the numbered Air Force. In addition to all this, there is a public address system, wherein SAC can vocally alert each unit to an urgent message. Teleprinters are in evidence, one that teletypes messages to and from SAC (for documentation and verification), a direct line to the weather office that constantly updates weather sequences for all SAC bases, plus several recorders, that document every conversation.

The conference room had a full view of the huge plexiglass display board in front of the controllers. On it was the number of each aircraft in the Wing, its status, the crew flying it, its location, and the basic mission profile. Everything revolves about the Wing Command Post, and at this time the amount of activity was unusual. We were shortly to find out why.

* * * *

"Coffee, gentlemen? Good. Sergeant, three cups, please. OK, now, Dave (another shock, he never called anyone by their first name), I want a complete recap of your mission. Don't leave anything out. You two," he motioned to the perplexed Harry and bored Bob," Chime in whenever you have something to add. Sergeant, start the machine," as he gestured towards a tape recorder, sitting on the long, massive conference table.

"Colonel, before we say anything, and before you start that damned thing, I want to know what the hell's going on."

"OK, I'm sorry. Sergeant, turn off the recorder. You are excused. I'll call you when I want you." The airman reluctantly departed, shutting the conference room door behind him. We were alone.

"Now, first things first. What I'm going to tell you is not to leave this room. Do you understand?" All three of us nodded, none of us having the slightest idea of what was going on. The warmth and closeness of the room perpetuated our grogginess and not thinking clearly.

"You are the only ones who made it around the horn. Between the 68th and us, 78 B-47s left England and so far 30 have returned there, unable to get their fuel. We got the word 12 have reached the states and landed all over the northern tier of bases, one at Barksdale from the 68th. That leaves 34 unaccounted for, and you. SAC is jumping up and down. We'll find them, but you're the only ones we have been able to talk to, so...."

"Colonel, four more accounted for," came over the loudspeaker. "Three at Selfridge (Michigan), one at Plattsburgh (New York)." The Colonel made some fast calculations. 31 still out. My God, I thought, this was really a fiasco. Not enough of them "played it by ear," obviously

Putting down his pencil, he continued. "Communications has been spotty in the UK, so we can hope more are there. The tanker reports read like a nightmare. SAC has put a total security blanket on Texas League, and I've got to get your story in detail. The CINC

(Commander-in-Chief) is wanting some answers and fast. Now, are you ready to give me the details?"

The full impact of what had happened and how fate thrust us into the midst of the biggest failure in SAC's history hit me all of a sudden. I was to hate my part in this, but that was to come later.

"OK, Colonel, turn on the recorder. Bob, Harry, get your charts out, and we'll go through this, mile by mile. The paperwork shuffle was about to begin.

Our recapitulation took over two hours, and so many cups of coffee I lost count. We were getting so groggy I asked the Colonel for about 10 minutes to go outside and get some fresh air, hoping that would clear our heads. He agreed, but cautioned us not to talk to anyone while we were outside the conference room. Upon our return, the 68th DO came in, still in his flying suit, having driven from Barksdale, where he landed, too short on fuel to make it the last hundred miles. He patted me on the shoulder as he passed by and sat down in an empty seat next to me. He really looked exhausted and obviously worried about his "boys." He said nothing, rather listened to the remainder of our tale.

We wrapped things up, finally, and were told our "outstanding feat of airmanship" would be duly noted and to go home and get some sleep. We were not to discuss the mission with anyone and to report back to the CP at 4:00 p.m. It was now 6:00 a.m. We left our classified folders, maps and logs with the Duty Controller. As we were leaving, I noticed one of the controllers was making copies of our flight logs on the duplicating machine. At that point I was too tired to care.

Going home and sleep was still a long way off. The three of us silently walked the block and a half to squadron operations, dragging our flight gear. Coming to work were some of the base personnel, but there was a silence that was disturbing. As we approached our operations, I saw our solitary B-47 sitting on the ramp. A maintenance vehicle drove by. It seemed as though the driver was looking for someplace to go or something to do. I fleetingly wondered if Vince had gotten away from the maintenance people, or did he have to spend a lot of time explaining what had happened from his point of view?

The Squadron Duty Officer was waiting for us in the briefing room. The young lieutenant was on the phone as we entered. "Yes Sir, I understand. No Sir, I won't keep them long. Sir, they just came in and I'll get them out real quick. Yes, Sir. Good night, Sir."

After duty hours, each squadron has an officer on duty as long as any squadron crew is flying. Usually the duty officer is one of the new members who hasn't qualified in his crew position. This one must have had only two flights in the B-47, as I recalled. He flew with me once on an upgrading flight in the local area. Terry was an eager type and I felt he would be a good copilot once he settled down and became part of the system. His main problem was that as a young bachelor, he felt he had to prove the SAC system to all of the young Southern Louisiana maidens he could find.

Bob, Harry and I flopped down across the table from the young-ster and waited for him to start the debriefing. He obviously was flustered by the phone call. He messed up his neat piles of papers, trying to act like he knew what he was doing.

"Good morning, Major. Let's get on with this so you can get the hell out of here." My God, I thought. He's still eager after a long, frustrating night. It was so depressing I made no comment. Harry lit a cigarette and Bob nonchalantly started unlacing his hightop combat boots. I sighed.

Terry picked up his pencil. "Flight Log?"

"It's at the Wing Command Post with the Vice CO," Harry offered. Terry made a notation on the debriefing form. Very efficient.

"Radar Log?" Harry passed it across the table. Terry made a check mark on the form and placed the log ceremoniously in a manila folder.

"Gunnery Log?" Bob floated it in his direction. Another checkmark and another form in the folder.

"Aircraft status?"

"In commission." Another notation.

"Air Refueling?" I chuckled, and Bob made a choking sound. I answered "Yes. Onload 45,000 pounds, five wet contacts, 25 dry contacts, one radar rendezvous." Hurried notations.

"Intercepts?"

"Three attempts, but they didn't make it. Locations are on the flight log." Terry hesitated, scratched his head with the pencil, then entered the number of fighter intercepts in the appropriate space.

"Bomb runs?"

"One radar run. Bombs away time is on the radar log."

"Nav legs?"

"Four. Radar nav legs. No celestial legs."

"Flight time?"

"Twelve hours and 15 minutes."

"Any comments?" I knew that was coming, but couldn't think of anything I could say at this point, so I passed. Bob shook his head and Harry just looked at me.

"OK, you guys. Get out of here. I need to get my beauty sleep." His attempt at humor fell on deaf ears as we were already on our way to our lockers to stow our gear.

"Dave, you want to come over for breakfast. Margaret will be waiting up for me and won't mind?" Harry was really sincere with his offer and hard to refuse. But I just wasn't up to any social amenities after what we just went through. I couldn't unwind in front of Margaret. She wasn't familiar with Harry's business in any great detail, and would be embarrassed if we got involved in flight talk. I declined.

"I'll see you all at 4 o'clock," Bob said as he was walking out the door.

"OK, Bob. Harry, tell Margaret thanks for the invite, but I'm too dirty and want to take a shower." Harry nodded, smiled and waved as he left.

* * * *

The officers mess was open, so I had breakfast. As I was finishing my second cup of coffee and about to light a cigarette, the

Base Commander came by and sat down. He had flown with my crew once and I had taught him at the B-47 ground school lectures.

"Morning, Dave. The base sure is quiet. Heard you come in, but that's all. Must have been a real roughy, right?" The Colonel always spoke in short, clipped sentences. You had to really listen closely or you would miss what he was saying.

"You bet, Colonel. I don't know where the rest of the troops are, but I imagine there'll be a whole task force back in England."

"I left the CP before they got your ETA (estimated time of arrival) transmitted from Chicago Center when we gave it to them. I thought nobody made it. Understand one 68th bird landed at Barksdale. Several at Forbes. Thank God no one went down."

Everyone liked this Base Commander. His function was to service the bomb wings and air refueling squadrons; he took an active interest in the flight crews even though that wasn't his job. On a USCM he always was in the Command Post of one of the wings, helping whenever and however he could.

"Colonel, I'm glad to hear that, but whoever made the decision at SAC to launch us with that crappie weather over Greenland ought to have been there. I hope to hell he has a lot of sleepless nights." I probably overstepped my bounds, but I just didn't care.

"Dave, you know better. Don't sweat it. They'll learn from their mistakes."

"Maybe so, but those bastards didn't have to put us into that kind of a position. It's hard to pass it off, particularly when you're on the tail-end of the stick."

"Go home, Dave. Unwind. SAC will talk to you this afternoon." "Yeah, maybe by then they will have a logical excuse for this fiasco, but I doubt it. Hey, don't mind me, Colonel. I just got to get this off my chest. It's pretty heavy."

The Base Commander nodded, got up, and left for his office. My blowing off steam didn't help. I was still mad, and probably would be for some time to come.

* * * *

By the time I was due at the Command Post I had partially settled down and had decided to keep my mouth shut for a change. Harry was already there, looking well rested, and in a neatly pressed uniform. Bob walked in right behind me, looking a disheveled as ever and needing a shave.

"Dave," greeted the Vice Commander, "you and your boys have got SAC in an uproar! I've had to deliver a copy of your flight log to them by T33 this morning. They don't believe you flew the route as briefed." He was excited and his words tumbled out in rapid succession. As Harry started out of his chair, I put my hand on his arm and he relaxed, but I could feel the tension in his muscles.

"Colonel, from where we sit, SAC wouldn't believe anything if you presented it to them on a silver tray. They're looking for a pigeon and I'm here to tell you we were a maximum of 20 miles off course the whole route, and that was because the jet stream blew us off course before we reached coast-in in Canada. If they want proof, send the radar photography to SAC. But I'll tell you this my crew will expect an apology when it's over." I was really wound up all over again, and, in retrospect, I wouldn't have blamed the Colonel if he had come down on me hard. But he didn't.

"Settle down Dave. I'm on your side. SAC is under the gun from the CINCSAC. You're being the only one who made it home stands out like a sore thumb. The Old Man is already at SAC, along with the DO. I've been on the squak box with him all morning. Good God, man, do you think I don't know what's going on? You're the only one who made it around the horn. SAC has over a hundred B-47s scattered all over hell and gone. The only reason they're questioning you is you're the only one who made it. I don't agree with them, but I can understand, considering the position they're in."

"Colonel," I cut in," the only thing I know is I flew their damned mission as briefed, and flew it even though I knew their decision was stupid. And what did it get me, but a kick in the butt!"

"Dave, settle down and let me handle it from here. I've recalled the Standboard Navigator and he's replotting your radar film right now. Once I get that I'll shove it down their throat and with pleasure, that's a personal promise."

Harry later told me he had already thought of that, but didn't mention it at the time because he was enjoying himself watching me "perform." I almost blew a gasket at the time.

The radar set in SAC bombers has a camera and film installed for each mission. The camera films the radar picture and is used primarily to aid radar operators in reviewing radar bomb runs and scoring techniques, but the camera is also used on USCMs to plot navigation legs, turning points, etc. After the mission aircraft lands, the photo people remove the used film cartridges, process it and send it to the Wing Navigators office for review. Although I had implicit faith in Harry's navigation, I also had my flight log and map that I used to cross-check our position. I used radio beams for fixes and annotated Harry's positions on my charts. I held this trump card in reserve and said nothing about it.

"Spiral Control, this is Buster, over." The public address system startled me, and I involuntarily flinched. The duty controller answered the call from SAC Headquarters, whose call sign was Buster.

"Roger, Buster. This is Spiral Control. Over."

"Spiral, this is Buster. Is the acting Commander there? Over."

"Roger, Buster." He looked back over his shoulder at Pyle, who nodded.

"Spiral, he's going to get a call on the scrambler. Have him standby. Over."

"Roger, Buster. Standing by." "Colonel, the call will be on the green phone. You can take it in the conference room if you like."

"Thanks. I'll take it here." He turned to me and explained. "This'll be a call from the Old Man. He's been with the SAC DO (Director of Operations) since early this morning. Maybe we'll hear something. At last count, we're still in the dark about the whereabouts of three birds, but..." The green phone rang and he picked it up.

"Yes, Rip, on scrambler. OK, I've got them here, now.

"No, nothing from photo interpretation." Pause.

"I understand. The AC's damned mad and I don't blame him. SAC knows better than to question this Lead crew." Another pause.

"That's right, boss." Another pause. "OK, I'll tell them."

"I'm glad to get the word about the three. "We'll notify the squadrons that they'll be in tomorrow. A long pause.

"Yes, sir. If you need transport, let me know. I've got a T-33 (single engine jet training aircraft) standing by. Good luck." He hung up, and turned to us with a smile on his weary face. Obviously an explanation was about to come.

"You're off the hook. The Old Man's talked to NORAD (North American Defense Command) and got the time and location of the B-47 that alerted the Air Defense. It was Jackson with our DO (Finan) aboard. They couldn't get enough fuel, so they cut some corners, and that's how NORAD was alerted. Bernie's in big trouble from the sound of the Old Man's voice." That figures, I thought. He was the same clown who said "play it by ear," when asked what we'd do if we couldn't get any fuel. I still can't stand that phrase.

"Oh, by the way, if it's of any consequence, the boss sends his regrets and SAC, also. You're in the clear. May even get a citation." He looked me straight in the eye, expecting what, I didn't know.

"Thanks, Colonel, but I'm afraid none of the three of us are likely to extend ourselves the way we did last night, again. My people are professionals and act like it. You can't do what SAC accused us of and expect us to forget that easily." I knew I was about to get in over my head, but a glance at Harry and Bob showed me I was expressing their feelings, also. With that I figured I'd better get it all out. "Colonel, I don't know whether you remember it or not, but the three of use went from Non-Ready to

Lead in a record time, passed SES (Strategic Evaluation Squadron, where every crew that is scheduled for high priority wartime targets gets evaluated under the most grueling and strict standards), and have led the wing in both bombing, air refueling and navigation for the past nine months. I'm sorry, maybe we're too proud, but we're treated like we're guilty until proved innocent. SAC wants a scapegoat, and we were it. I'm sorry, but that's one damned bitter pill to swallow. We're supposed to smile and go on our way. I don't know, Colonel, maybe we can act like professionals, but I haven't spent seven years busting my butt for SAC to be treated this way." I was through, but I could have said a lot more. Bob later said he expected me to be relieved right there, and Harry said I echoed his thoughts exactly, but would never have had the guts to come right out and say it.

"All right, Dave. Do what you think is best. I can't say anything more. You're dismissed." He stared at me for what seemed like an eternity, then got up and walked out of the room.

* * * *

We left our classified folders, maps and logs with the Command Post Senior Controller. The three of us went our own ways with our own thoughts. Nothing needed to be said between us. We knew we had done our job and would be able to have personal satisfaction knowing no one else had flown Texas League "as briefed." None of us would ever forget those 12 hours. Even now I vividly remember each phase of it. I will always remember Harry Reitan and Bob Tanner and their part in the whole fiasco. We split up the same year. Harry went on to get his master's degree and PhD, Bob got his own crew. I've lost track of them, but not their deeds, or their friendship.

Chapter 30

POST MORTEM

Our crew flew three more Pop-Ups and became the first crew to be "qualified" for low level operation. There was one more route, called Whiskey Red, that we never flew as a crew. It was a long flight (by comparison with Orange and Blue) and went from Lake Charles and bombed Dallas.

After becoming qualified on November 27, 1957, I flew with various crews to get them qualified (the copilot stayed home). For some it was easy, for some it was very tough, and some of the crews never got the hang of the techniques and flying low level. Some of the navigators couldn't find the target in such a short bomb run and would not get a creditable score. Those people were transferred or replaced and underwent more training. I flew a total of 23 Pop-Ups, and enjoyed every minute of it. I firmly believe low level in a B-47 was a lot mental and a small amount of physical dexterity.

The bright spot of our crew activities was when we were selected to drop a Mark 36 nuclear training weapon. It was painted blue, shaped like a real 10,000 pound nuclear bomb. It was called Operation Straight Shot and involved flying to the Eglin AFB Test Range, in northwest Florida at Range #70, and releasing the weapons at low level and, as usual, 425 knots. We were to contact Range Control as we passed south of Eglin AFB, and descend to 10,000 feet.

We monitored the installation of the weapon on a non-wing tank aircraft (52-590). On June 19, 1959 we tookoff, climbed to 33,000 feet and headed for Eglin over the Gulf of Mexico. To my surprise, the Range Controller answered our call the first time and asked if we were on a heading of 070 and south of Eglin. We were. The Controller, directing us, told us to descend to 2,000 feet over the Gulf on our present heading, and then to orbit east of Panama City until "they" were ready for us. As we passed 10,000 feet, we were told to turn north and descend to 500 feet. We complied.

"We have you. Descent to 500 feet, and turn left to a heading of 270. We will advise you when to start your bomb run. Your radar operator will be able to see the target as you start your climb to 18,000 feet. When you release your bomb, start an immediate 45 degree turn to the left and climb to 35,000 feet. We will let you know when you have reached the Initial Point. Start your climb at that point. Do you understand?"

"Roger, we understand. Standing by for IP." I knew Harry was listening and asked him if he "had" the target. He rogered me and said there was nothing on his radar. I knew this was probable, because there were no reflecting targets in the vicinity of our bomb run. Northwestern Florida is nothing but sand and pine trees.

"Over your IP, Blast 43, start your climb, now. Do you have the target?" Harry said he was picking up what looked like a cross(metal), and to engage the autopilot and give him control, which I did. Harry had the target and it showed two degrees right. The aircraft followed and I reached 18,000 feet and maintained 425 knots. The "time to go" meter showed 60 seconds.

"Are you OK, Harry?" He said yes and I informed Eglin Control we had 45 seconds. They said that was fine, and call them at "Bombs Away."

"30 seconds, Harry. Stand by for a maximum rate turn."

"Roger, I have the target. You can't miss it, from here." The bomb doors opened at 10 seconds, automatically.

"Bombs Away," I yelled and started a 45 degree turn, advanced the throttles, pulled the nose up and we went up like the proverbial rocket.

"We got a direct hit. That ought to satisfy them," yelled Harry, as we passed through 15,000 feet, and I rolled out on a southern heading, continuing our climb to 35,000 feet.

"Blast 43, good hit. You can go home, now." I tried to contact them, but they did not answer.

SAC changed the wing designators normally every six months. Blast changed to Buddy. It was that simple. That was our last mission, together. It was a good run and we set a standard that would be hard to beat.

Chapter 31

EPILOGUE

In retrospect, the temporary change from high to low altitude for the strategic bomber fleet was understandable but the adjustment left a lot to be desired in the way it was ill-planned and the routes pushed us to the limit, and beyond. The careers of whom the government spent an inordinate amount of money to train, was not a good decision to make. Longer training and more intense crew coordination would have been a much better way to get a "qualified" crew. It stretched the capability of the less experienced crews, the ones who needed the confidence.

Keep in mind, the factual story derived from my personal note and flight logs, took place in the early 1950s when there was no experience in low level high speed bombing, no satellites, no GPS (Ground position system); refueling was by slow prop-driven tankers and very few of the Wing Staff had any experience in flying jet bombers.

The requirement to train pilots to be bombardiers, navigators and radar operators was timely, and, I firmly believe, made better pilots. Unfortunately, the B-47 was replaced by the B-52 with the multi-crew operational concept, and the "four-headed monsters" concept was abandoned. It was still an excellent idea, making the crew pilots understand the problems of the other crew members.

The problems we experienced in Korea and Vietnam were not caused by the military and local governments. Rather, the politicians were, and are, the culprits of the mess this country has gotten itself into.

We are not respected, and only recently have the veterans of the two fracas been given, begrudgingly, the minimum of understanding of what the military was required to do. The use of ground troops who couldn't protect themselves for fear of "upsetting" the Chinese. The Korean War was a war we were not allowed to win. The Congress and the President didn't learn from that (and it was repeated again in Vietnam, and on a much larger scale in the form of human loss). It's a sad commentary that we got involved in either war, but once we got into it, the criticism was against the military, those who were shackled and ignored. We could not win.

More recently, and at a much higher cost, was Vietnam. We weren't allowed to bomb Hanoi, or Haiphong, and we couldn't mine the Haiphong harbor, where the majority of equipment was sent to aid the Communists in north Vietnam. We couldn't bomb the trucks coming in from China. When we flew out of Bien Hoa on our test flights with the U-2R, the missions were always over the North Vietnam/China border, Hanoi or Haiphong. The resultant photographs only verified what we already know. It was a war we couldn't win, the congress and the President didn't react.

The use of the B-52 was a farce. We didn't have any legitimate targets in North Korea. In Vietnam the B-52 was launched out of Thailand and they were used without benefit of priority targets. Another case of misuse of equipment at the expense of the taxpayer. So it was another classic example of not being able to win, but we were in it, and, again, you don't go to war not expecting to try to win.

This book was not written to be critical of the decision makers, but when they make the same mistake twice, one has to consider why they don't learn. The American serviceman paid the price with their lives for the backbone of the politicians.

Texas League and Whiskey Orange are history, but you won't find the results in any of SAC historical publications available to the public. The big boss at SAC called in all the Wing Commanders of Texas League and I understand they came away feeling like they had been hit by a steamroller. There never was any critique of the crews, but we pieced together the facts. Of the 78 that were launched from England, 19 reached the United States, and only one got back to its home base. I've lived with those statistics for many years and hated it every time they came into my mind. I felt, and still do, that the Strategic Air Command literally stands between us and disaster. It was, and is, a force that is made up of professionals who put their life on the line every day. Outside of the Command, they get little enough recognition, and, as a result, the quality of the crews has deteriorated. The lack of discipline is the major cause for this decline. This is not SAC's fault. Rather, it is the permissiveness thrust upon the military by outside forces.

If it ever comes to a showdown, God forbid, I fervently hope that professional pride will outweigh the social permissive attitudes. If not, we're in big trouble.

As I look back on my seven years of flying the B-47, I feel an overwhelming sense of pride and sorrow. It is with pride that I remember those who made SAC what it is; it is with sorrow I remember that the B-47 is no longer with us. After over 2,000 flying hours in jets, my memory still is strong and factually supplemented by my flight logs. She was more than an airplane; she was more than a weapon; she was a love that will last.

* * * *

When I first began this story, I was hoping the events that took place would show how a series of events and poor decisions would spell disaster, even to a corps of professionals. Now, I hope it will have a deeper meaning. The age of the Intercontinental Ballistic Missile is here, and near cancellation of the B-1 bomber program is an incursion into the safety of the American people.

The present strategic bomber fleet is now more than 20 years old, and, as each year passes, the numbers of the only flexible deterrent force dwindles. The ICBM was designed for nuclear war and can only deliver a nuclear weapon. While we are reducing our strategic aircraft inventory, the anti-Americans are building a strategic bomber force at an alarming rate. Conventional war waged against the United States would favor the enemy, for we could not use our ICBM's for fear of their counterparts being used against us. Even if the government realized the danger of our reduced defensive posture, it would be at least five years before we could regain equality.

Other books written by the author:

Reconnaissance is Black
Escape or Evade?
Highway to Freedom
Texas League
Whiskey Orange

www.ingramcontent.com/pod-product-compliance
Lightning Source LLC
LaVergne TN
LVHW041152080426
835511LV00006B/570